AF479142

GHYCZY

[gɪt|siː]

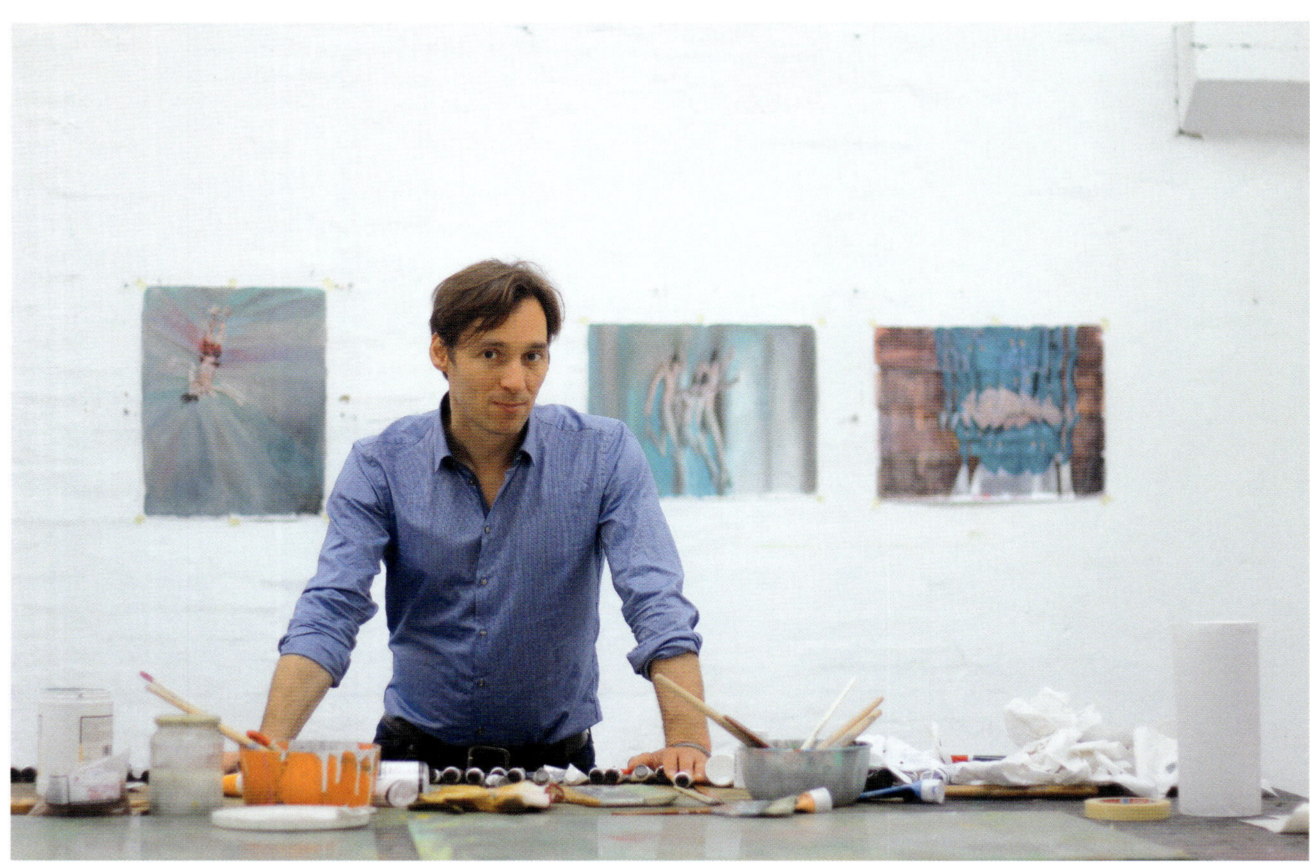

Studio, Budapest 2014

DÉNESH GHYCZY

BETWEEN LINES

KERBER ART

Sven Grünwitzky

AUFGEHENDE AUGEN

„Der König Ödipus hat ein Auge zu viel vielleicht.“ (Hölderlin)

OPENING EYES

„Perhaps King Oedipus has an eye too many.“ (Hölderlin)

Wie viele Gesichter hat das Gegenüber, wie viele Augen der Betrachter?

Sehen ist mitnichten eine Selbstverständlichkeit. Auch angesichts der neuerlichen Entfesselungsstufe des Visuellen im digitalen Äther ist keineswegs ausgemacht, dass wir nur zu sehen begonnen hätten. Mehr zu sehen zu bekommen, bedeutet nicht, *mehr* zu sehen. Vielleicht verlieren wir unter dem Druck der unzähligen Bilder sogar wesentliche Dimensionen des Sehens buchstäblich aus den Augen, wenn unsere im medientechnologischen Gebrauch geschulte Visualität die Leistung unserer Augen auf eine effiziente Reizverarbeitung optischer Signale reduziert. Wir halten damit die Tätigkeit der Augen an der kurzen Leine, begrenzen sie auf die Verarbeitung von Sinnesdaten oder fassen sie als passives Einfallstor des Erlebens auf.

Unter allem, was wir sehen, liegt zunächst die einfache Tatsache, dass wir sehen. Aber was bedeutet Sehen überhaupt? Wie wird sichtbar, was wir sehen? Können wir mit bloßen Augen verstehen? Wie eigenständig sind unsere Augen, und von welchem Ort aus sehen wir, wenn wir sehen? Ist es möglich, uns vor Augen zu führen, dass wir sehen? Erschöpft sich Sehen im Erkennen des Sichtbaren? Können wir nur Objekte der äußeren Wirklichkeit sichten? Oder sehen wir sogar besser mit geschlossenen Augen? Gibt es so etwas wie ein geistiges Auge? Und welche Rolle spielen in diesen Angelegenheiten die weiten Oberflächen des Bildlichen als eine von der unmittelbaren Gegebenheit der sichtbaren Dinge emanzipierten Form?

Die Bilder des ungarisch-deutschen Malers Dénesh Ghyczy führen uns immer wieder neu vor Augen, dass das Wahrnehmungsfeld des Sehens eine oszillierende Angelegenheit sein kann und weit mehr umfasst als das, was wir auf den ersten Blick zu sehen meinen. Auf unterschied-

How many eyes look at how many faces?

Seeing is something we really should not take for granted. We should not even assume that we have learned how to see, despite the flood of visuals we are presented with in the digital ether. Having more to see does not mean we see more. In fact, the pressure from these innumerable images might even mean we are literally losing sight of important aspects of seeing. After all, if our visuality is being trained by or in the use of media technology, it could be the case that the performance of our eyes is being reduced to the efficient processing of optical stimuli. This would be like keeping our eyes on a short leash, limiting their role to processing sensory data. Or treating them merely as a passive, open hatch through which life's real experiences pass.

Underlying everything that we see is the main, simple fact that we see. But what does seeing mean anyway? How does what we see become visible? Can we understand with the naked eye? How independent are our eyes and what place do we see from when we see? Is it possible for someone to make us see that we are seeing? Is recognizing the visible all there is to seeing? Can we only see objects of external reality? Or do we, in fact, see better when our eyes are closed? Is there such a thing as a third or inner eye? And what is the role being played within these considerations by the broad expanses of artistic imagery—emancipated as it is from the immediacy of visible things?

The paintings of the Hungarian-German painter Dénesh Ghyczy keep reminding us anew how the perceptual field of seeing can be an oscillating affair, encompassing far more than what we think we see at first glance.

lichen Wegen lenkt er unsere Betrachtung auf die Schauplätze des Sehens. Er zeigt, dass wir mehr als zwei Augen brauchen, um zu sehen, und dass wir schon im Akt des Sehens das bloß Sichtbare hinter uns lassen.

Mit Blick auf das Universum seiner Bilder erscheint in den Augenwinkeln des Betrachters außerdem ein weiter Kreis von Themen und Motiven, welche den Augensinn mit der Frage des Bildes und den grundlegenden Selbstbetrachtungen des Menschen zusammenschließt: die enge Verbindung von Augen und Händen im Akt von Sehen und Begreifen; die trügerischen Schattenspiele der Täuschung; das Verhältnis von Illusion, Evidenz und Blindheit, welche die Ungewissheiten der Sinne begleiten; die vibrierenden Momente und stillstehenden Augenblicke in den sehnsüchtigen Versuchen menschlicher Selbstvergewisserung.

All diese Felder erkundet Ghyczy auf dem Weg der Malerei. Einer Malerei, der nichts Konzeptionelles anhaftet, bleibt sie doch – das sei vorausgeschickt – immer beim Sichtbaren und Gegenständlichen, zumeist auch der menschlichen Figur; jedoch nie, ohne diese physische Zone in einem bestimmten Sinn auch wieder zu überschreiten oder hinter sich zu lassen. Und wenngleich sich seine Malerei in diesem Transzendieren des Sichtbaren in einem ständigen medialen Wechselspiel mit der Fotografie befindet, fließt sie doch letztlich immer wieder zurück in den unmittelbaren und handwerklich eloquent vorgetragenen Umgang mit Pinsel, Farbe und Leinwand.

Vielleicht kann man so weit gehen zu behaupten, dass Malerei grundsätzlich ihre Gegenstände erst ausmalen muss, um sie bildlich erscheinen zu lassen, weil sie nicht über die Neutralität der Mittel verfügt, die Dinge abzubilden, wie es die Fotografie durch ihren optischen Automatismus beherrscht. Ausmalen bedeutete dann, den Gegenstand des Bildes über das Handwerkliche der Pinselführung und das

In a variety of ways he directs us to consider the locations of seeing. He shows us that we need more than two eyes to see, and that we leave the simply visible behind as soon as we engage in the act of seeing.

By looking at the universe of his paintings, the observer will notice out of the corner of their eye a wide circle of topics and motifs which bring together our power of sight with the whole issue of "a picture" and the fundamental self-observations of humanity: the close link between eyes and hands in the act of seeing and grasping; the deceptive shadow play of illusions; the relationship between illusion, evidence, and blindness, which accompanies the uncertainties of the senses; and the vibrating moments and motionless instances of a human's longing attempts at self-assurance.

Painting is the path Ghyczy has chosen to explore these fields. His paintings cannot be fixed within a particular concept but—and we do need to state this in advance—it does always stay within the realm of the visible and tangible. This generally means the human figure. Nonetheless, it never fails to go beyond or leave behind this physical realm in some way or another. And even though in this transcendence of the visible his style embraces a constant medial interplay with photography, it always eventually flows back into the direct and practically eloquent manner with which he uses his brush, paint, and canvas.

Perhaps we can go so far as to say it is a fundamental requirement of the medium of painting in first envisioning its subject. Otherwise the subject cannot appear as an image, since this medium does not enjoy the neutrality of portrayal which photography does, thanks to its optical automatism. Here, envisioning means taking the subject of the picture and having it appear in a rhetorical and transfigurative sense, well beyond the practical brushstrokes and the immediacy of the visible subject.

Augenscheinliche des sichtbaren Objekts hinaus in einem rhetorischen und transfigurativen Sinn erscheinen zu lassen.

Um sich auszumalen, braucht Malerei zudem Zeit, deren Vergehen sie in das Bild einarbeitet. Nach heutigem Empfinden ist sie deshalb ein geradezu quälend langsames Geschäft – und ein recht umständliches und eigentlich unangemessen aufwendiges Verfahren, um Dinge der sichtbaren Wirklichkeit abzubilden, würde sie dem Sichtbaren in ihrer Arbeit am Material nicht zusätzliche Erfahrungswerte hinzufügen. Malerei formt im Medium des Bildes eine Synergie aus den Möglichkeiten des Sehens, Hörens und Fühlens, das Surplus einer Textur aus Lauschen, Berühren und Begehren. Und sie vermag es, sich mit ihren Mitteln gleichsam frei im Sichtbaren zu bewegen.

Malerei also verlangsamt das Sehen. So verlangen auch die Gemälde von Dénesh Ghyczy dem Betrachter die Geduld ab, das Auge als tastendes Organ zu erfahren, es schweifen und schauen zu lassen. Es in den Zwischenräumen von Wahrnehmen und Erkennen, von Malerei und Fotografie, von Gestalt und Abstraktion zu bewegen, um nicht nur die sichtbaren Gegenstände, sondern auch die Erfahrung der Augen auf den Bildflächen aufgehen zu lassen. Unter Umständen werden sich dabei die betrachteten Gesichter des Gegenübers vervielfältigen, oder dem Betrachter gehen gar mehr als nur die zwei leiblichen Augen auf.

Linsen und Visionen

Dénesh Ghyczy hat in seinen Arbeiten der vergangenen beiden Jahrzehnte immer wieder die Zusammenhänge des Sichtbaren malerisch neu erkundet, indem er das Gesehene als Produkt der Augen und die Malerei als bildliches Erzeugnis hinterfragt.

Systematisch nutzte er anfangs die Gesetze der Lichtbrechung, um

For this, painting also needs time; the passing of time then also becomes worked into the picture. In today's world this makes painting feel like an almost tortuously slow affair. In fact, we can agree that painting would be a fairly inconvenient and unnecessarily involved process for depicting the objects of visible reality if it did not supplement the purely visible with additional experiential value during that process. Within the medium of the picture, painting creates a synergy from the opportunities of seeing, hearing, and feeling—a surplus from the textures of listening, touching, and desiring. And painting is capable of using its resources to move freely within the visible realm, so to speak.

So painting decelerates our seeing. The paintings of Dénesh Ghyczy certainly demand patience from their observers: the patience they need to experience their eye as an organ of exploration and let it wander and take things in. By moving in the spaces between perception and recognition, painting and photography, or form and abstraction, the artist is able to transfer not only the visible subject matter, but also the experience of opening the eyes onto the canvas. In some cases, the face we are looking at is duplicated or in others we find ourselves looking with more than merely our two physical eyes.

Lenses and Visions

In his works of the past two decades, Dénesh Ghyczy has conducted new artistic explorations of the contexts of the visible realm by questioning our assumptions that what we see is a product of our eyes and that painting is a pictorial product.

Initially he used the laws of refraction to undermine the apparent obviousness of visibility. While making a photographic image of a per-

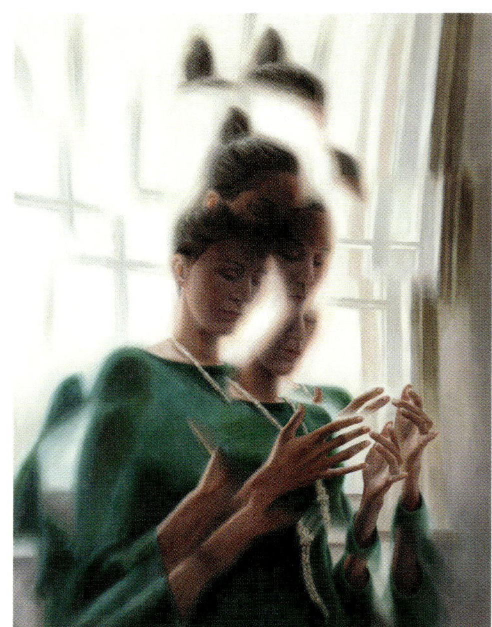

Mind-Body (Gwen)
2012, 140 x 105 cm, oil on canvas

die Selbstverständlichkeit des Sichtbaren zu unterlaufen. Während der fotografischen Ablichtung verstellte er die Sicht auf sein Gegenüber mit unterschiedlichen Gläsern und Linsen. So erzeugte er fotografische Matrizen von Freunden und Bekannten, die sich dem Diktat der Wiedererkennung widersetzen. Bei der Übertragung der fotografischen Vorlage auf die Leinwand erlaubte ihm dieses Vorgehen, die Gesichter und Körper der Porträtierten mit den visuellen Effekten der Linsen und Scheiben in eine eigenständige Struktur der malerischen Darstellung zu übersetzen. [1]

Die so entstandenen Bilder irritieren den Blick des Betrachters. Sie verunsichern die gewöhnliche Seherfahrung, weil das Motiv in einem Moment gebannt ist, bevor das ordnende Erkennen die Eindrücke in einen vertrauten Gegenstand verwandeln kann. Als ob ein Störsender durch das Bild läuft, scheinen in manchen dieser Gemälde die Porträtierten in optische Sequenzen zerlegt: Gesichter werden fragmentiert und facettiert, Körper periodisch in Schwingung versetzt. Mal kräuselt sich ein Motiv wie im bewegten Spiel spiegelnder Wasseroberflächen, mal zergliedert ein geriffeltes Glasornament das menschliche Angesicht in repetitive Muster. In einigen Bildern dominiert das kühle Kalkül automatisierter Abstraktion, während andere den gesetzten Verfahrensrahmen mit leichter Hand wieder auflösen.

Altmeisterlich muten dagegen auf den ersten Blick die Bilder der Serie *Silent Mantras* an. Wieder zeigt Ghyczy uns Freunde und Bekannte, doch dieses Mal sind ihre Körper wie durch fotografische Mehrfachbelichtung vervielfältigt und dann in einer Art magischem Realismus effektvoll ineinandergearbeitet. Nie kommt der Sehsinn hier endgültig zur Ruhe. Je länger und intensiver das Auge betrachtet, umso mehr löst sich die feste Gestalt der Figuren in einer vibrierenden Vervielfältigung der Sinneseindrücke auf. Und doch scheinen die Personen, wie auch die

son he distorted the view with a range of glass types and lenses. In this way he created photographic matrices of friends and acquaintances which contradict the expectation of recognizability. Then, while transferring this photographic template onto canvas, his process allowed him to take the visual effects from the lenses and glass panes on the faces and bodies of the people in his portraits and translate them into an independent structure of artistic depiction. [1]

The pictures arising in this way interfere with the observer's view, confusing us and upsetting our usual experience of seeing, since the theme is frozen before the ordering process of recognition can transform the impressions into a familiar object. As if a source of interference had disrupted a broadcast, in some of the pictures the portrayed figures seem to be dissembled into optical sequences: faces are fragmented and faceted, bodies are set into periodic vibration. Sometimes a motif will ripple like the dynamic play of reflective water surfaces. Sometimes a ribbed glass ornament will dissect the human face into a repetitive pattern. In some pictures the dominant aspect is the cool calculation of automated abstraction, whereas others easily dissolve any established process.

At first glance, the series *Silent Mantras* has a touch of the Old Masters. Once again, Ghyczy shows us friends and acquaintances, but this time their bodies have been duplicated by multiple photographic exposures. Then a type of magical realism has been applied to work them together in an impressive way that never lets our visual sense ever really come to rest. As our eye considers the picture longer and more intensely, the solid forms of the figures dissolve into a vibrating duplication of sensory impressions. Nonetheless, the people and the paintings themselves, such as *Mind-Body (Gwen)*, 2012, or *Ksenia*, 2011, seem to become ever more vital when, as in a dream collage, deep trance or vision, the in-

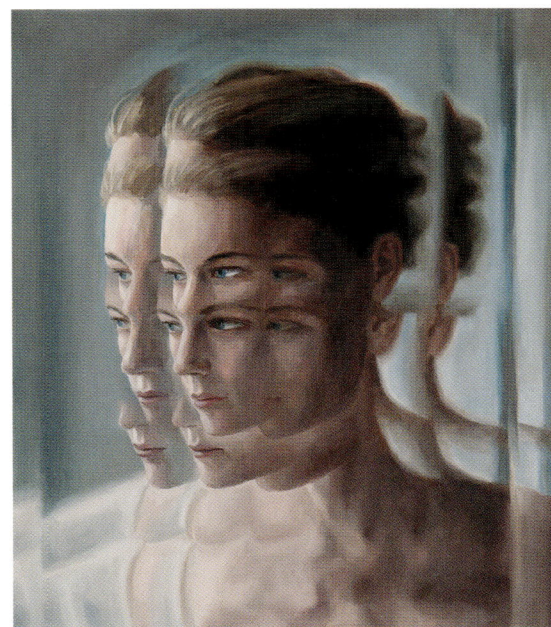

Ksenia
2011, 70 x 60 cm, oil on canvas

Bilder selbst, *Mind-Body (Gwen),* 2012, oder *Ksenia,* 2011, immer lebendiger zu werden, wenn die ineinandergeblendeten Körper, Hände und Gesichter wie in einem Traumgebilde, einer tiefen Trance oder Vision sich in pulsierende Bildtiefen hinein öffnen, in denen Raum- und Zeiterfahrung sich vermischen. Geisterhaft fließen auf anderen Gemälden dieser Serie mehrere Köpfe derselben Person ineinander oder es löst sich ein zweites Gesicht wie ein zarter Seelenhauch vom physischen Körper ab, so bei *I am, I am, I am,* 2012; *Shadow (Salila),* 2012.

Eindringlich finden sich in den changierenden Sinneseindrücken spirituelle Entgrenzungserfahrungen mit der zeitlichen Sequenzierung der Fotografie in einer detailtreuen Malerei vermählt.[2] So eng diese Bilder auf den ersten Blick am Motiv geführt werden und so konventionell sie als Gemälde zunächst gearbeitet scheinen, beunruhigen auch sie den wiedererkennenden Augensinn und richten den Blick durch das Gegebene und über das Sichtbare hinaus. Manchmal scheint es sogar, als ob sich etwas vom Geist des Gegenübers im Bild verfängt, gerade weil die primäre körperliche Einheit der Person sich in überblendenden Momentaufnahmen und mehrfachen Ansichten auflöst.

Der Griff in den blinden Bildgrund

Dem trüben Blick hilft keine Brille, benennt ein Sprichwort die Undurchsichtigkeit alles Geistlosen. Sehen meint nicht stumpfes Glotzen, sondern fordert wache Betrachtung. Weder führt Sichtbares ins Vorhersehbare noch Blindheit immer in Vision. Und doch gibt es ein inneres Zusammenspiel von Sehen und Wissen, das in einen konstitutiven Verbund von Evidenz und Blindheit eingelassen ist.

Wir können nur etwas sehen, indem wir anderes ausblenden, sind blind für vieles, um weniges sehen zu können. Gewohnheitsblind sind

terwoven blend of bodies, hands, and faces produce vibrating depths in the image where our experiences of space and time merge into one another. In a ghostly way, other paintings of the same series show multiple heads of the same person flowing into each other, or a second face gently lifting away like a fleeting soul from its physical body: *I am, I am, I am,* 2012, and *Shadow (Salila),* 2012.

These changing sensory impressions hauntingly bring together—and faithfully reproduce the details of—spiritual experiences of ego dissolution and photographic temporal sequencing.[2] Although these pictures initially seem to stick closely to the motif and be painted in a very conventional way, they still unsettle our powers of recognition and direct our view beyond the visible and tangible. Sometimes it even seems as if something of the subject's spirit has been caught in the picture, especially because their primary, physical entity has dissolved into overlapping momentary snapshots and multiple views.

Reaching into the Picture's Blind Ground

An old German saying sums up how we cannot see without spirit: "Glasses cannot improve dim vision." Seeing does not mean blankly staring: seeing needs alert observation. The visible does not always lead to the predictable, nor does blindness always lead to vision. But there is nonetheless an inner interplay between seeing and knowledge, embedded within a constitutive coupling of evidence and blindness.

We can only see something by shutting out something else. We are blind to many things in order to be able to see a few. We are habitually blind if we see without realizing we are seeing. And if we really want to see, it is not enough simply to have our eyes open.

With his artistic explorations, Dénesh Ghyczy persistently disturbs

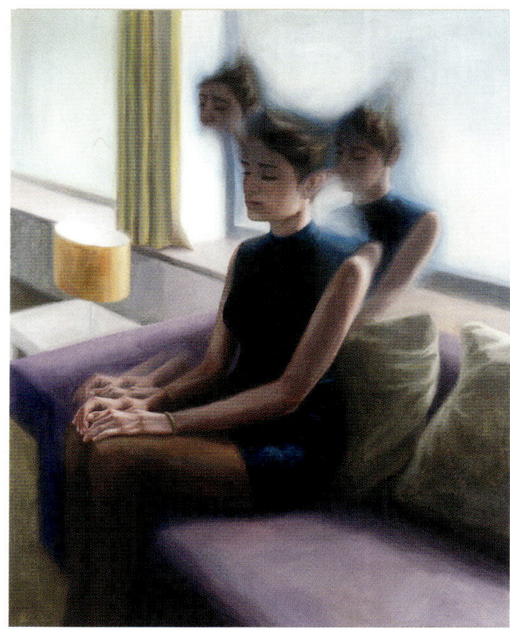

I Am, I Am, I Am
2012, 165 x 130 cm, oil on canvas

wir, wenn wir sehen, ohne es noch zu bemerken. Und um tatsächlich zu sehen, genügt es nicht, allein die Augen offen stehen zu haben.

Bei seinen malerischen Erkundungen rüttelt Dénesh Ghyczy hartnäckig an der Vertrautheit des Augensinns. Immer wieder führt uns sein Blick über die bloßen Daten der leiblichen Augen hinaus. Auch in den jüngeren Arbeiten wird die Selbstverständlichkeit der primären Seherfahrung aufgebrochen, nun fallen die Irritationen des Auges allerdings zurückgenommener und feinsinniger aus. Motiv und visueller Effekt sind nur noch selten zu einer bildlichen Einheit eingeschmolzen, stattdessen agieren die Figuren auf eigene Faust. Deutlich konturiert heben sich ihre Körper von den Untergründen ab. Figur und Grund, Gestalt und freie Malerei sind kontrastierend in eigenständige Geltungssphären auseinandergetreten. Ortlos stürzen vereinzelte Figuren durch undefinierte Farbräume oder zartgliedrige Pinsellasuren. Gesichter tauchen aus dichten Streifen oder energisch sich über die Bildfläche schlängelnden Pinselbahnen heraus auf. Subtil sind diese Figuren dabei mit den unterschiedlichen abstrakten Hintergründen ganz beiläufig verflochten oder hintergründig verstrickt. Und einige dieser Bilder geben in lebendig schwingender Malerei den Blick auf ihre Erscheinungen frei, als ob die breiten Pinselstriche frischen Tau von einer beschlagenen Scheibe nehmen würden. In diesen effektvollen Bildlösungen scheinen die Figuren ein ums andere Mal wie aus blinden Bildgründen, wie von Zauberhand aus dem Nichts heraus freigelegt zu sein. Die Malerei kreist hier um das Sichtbarwerden der Erscheinungen aus einem Feld des Unsichtbaren.

Manchmal lässt Ghyczy seine Figuren dabei behutsam Kontakt zu jener fremden Matrix der Bildgründe aufnehmen, deren entgrenztes All-over aus gestischen Farbströmen wie unbekannte Frequenzen, Strahlungen oder Energien den Bildraum in Schwingung versetzen.

the very familiarity of our sense of sight. Again and again, his perspective leads us beyond the mere data delivered by our physical eyes. His recent works also aim to stop us taking our primary visual experience for granted. However, the optical confusion that confronts our eyes has become more subtle and reserved. The motif and visual effect are now seldom merged into a pictorial unity; the figures are now acting of their own accord. The contours of their bodies stand out distinctly from the backgrounds. Figure and ground, form and free painting: these contrasts have diverged into their independent spheres of relevance. Unbound by place, individual figures blaze their way through undefined areas of color or glazes tenderly applied with the brush. Faces appear from dense stripes or brush strokes meandering rapidly across the painting's surface. Subtly, as if by chance, these figures are also weaved into or entangled with a variety of abstract backgrounds. And the vibrant technique of some of these pictures means they reveal their appearances to us as if the wide brushstrokes were wiping condensation from a fogged up windowpane early in the morning. These artistic ideas, full of affect, create an appearance of figures being magically set free or revealed out of blindness and void. In these paintings we experience how appearances become seeable out of the field of what we cannot see.

Ghyczy occasionally has his figures make careful contact with the unfamiliar matrix of the picture ground, whose delimiting all-over of sweeping color flows set the painting vibrating like unknown frequencies, rays, or energies. This can be seen in *Seeing Is Believing,* 2014, or *One Thought,* 2014, where his protagonists tentatively stretch their hands into the uncertainty of the broadly brushed image field.

What do their hands touch upon there? Does their uncertain reaching out also symbolize a blind person's experience of seeing, or that of the painter? After all, as modern art makes clear to us again and again,

Shadow (Salila)
2012, 140 x 105 cm, oil on canvas

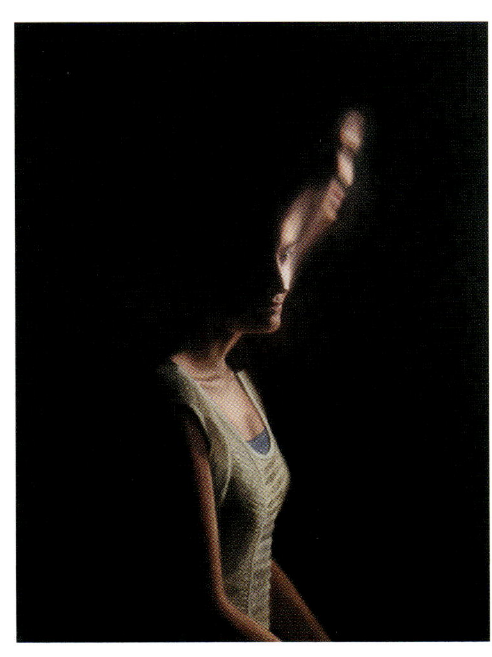

So greifen etwa in Seeing Is Believing oder One Thought, beide 2014, seine Protagonisten mit nestelnden Händen in die Ungewissheit einer solchen aus breiten Pinselstrichen geborenen Bildsphäre.

Was ertasten sie dabei? Sind in ihrem unsicheren Tasten nicht auch die Seherfahrung eines Blinden und damit zugleich auch diejenigen des Malers erfasst? Denn gleicht die Erfahrung des Malers, wie es uns auch die Erzählungen der modernen Kunst immer wieder nahelegen, nicht oft genug der eines Blinden, wenn er im Unbekannten des noch zu Findenden sein ‚Meisterwerk' sucht? [3]

Aufschlussreich scheint es aber auch, dieses Spiel der Finger in der abendländischen Darstellungstradition der Blindheit zu betrachten. Dort ersetzen zumeist tastende, weisende und zeigende Hände die mangelnde Sehkraft. Während in den Gesten der Blinden zumeist ein Zeichen für die gegenseitige Bedingtheit von Sehen, Begreifen und Erkennen formuliert ist, wird im Bild des Blinden zugleich die Ahnung einer dem Feld des Sichtbaren entzogenen Wahrnehmung erkennbar. Anschaulich wird dabei ein innerer Gedächtnis- und Erfahrungsraum, in dem der Blinde sich zu orientieren und mit geschärften Sinnen umsichtig zu handeln gelernt hat. Der Blinde benötigt keine Lampe, auch im Dunkeln nicht. Ausgerechnet an seinem Bildnis wird augenfällig, dass sich unser Sehen nicht im Gesehenen erschöpft. Philosophen von Platon bis Hegel haben deshalb mit dem Gedanken gespielt, dass das geistige Auge umso besser sieht, je mehr die leiblichen Augen geschlossen bleiben. [4]

Einzuwenden bliebe an dieser Stelle nur, dass solche aus den spekulativ abgedunkelten Innenräumen heraus entwickelten Impulse, die historisch fast immer auch augenkritisch und bilderfeindlich argumentierten, eine wesentliche Einsicht des Auges versäumen. Gerade eine ausgiebige und eindringliche Betrachtung von Bildern vermag die Augen darin zu schulen, nicht allein das zu sehen, was wir erwarten.

the experience of the artist is often similar to that of a blind person as he searches for his masterpiece in the unknown realm of the not-yet-found. [3]

We can surely gain some insight by considering this finger-play within the European tradition of portraying blindness, where tentative, indicative, and revelatory hands generally initially replace the missing power of vision. Although the gestures of the blind mostly indicate the mutual dependence of seeing, understanding, and recognizing, the image of the blind person does give us a hint of a perception that is removed from the field of the visible. An inner space then becomes vivid: a space of thoughts and experience in which a blind person finds orientation. They have learned to treat this space carefully with their heightened senses. A blind person needs no lamp, not even in the dark. In fact, it is the image of a blind person that helps us realize how our seeing is not only made up of what we actually see. From Plato to Hegel, many have played with the thought that an "inner eye" might see even better if our physical eyes are tightly shut. [4]

The only counterpoint to this is that these intuitions developed in speculative, darkened, internal spaces, historically almost always argue against the eyes and pictures, and neglect the essential insights of the eye. For through extensive, penetrating observation of pictures, we can school the eyes to see beyond what we expect.

Bell Jar

Dénesh Ghyczy seems to take the visible as a starting point for a journey into the inner spaces of our soul. In many of his pictures, his subjects have their eyes closed. They are listening inwardly, seeking contact to something that is not clearly portrayed in the picture itself. This some-

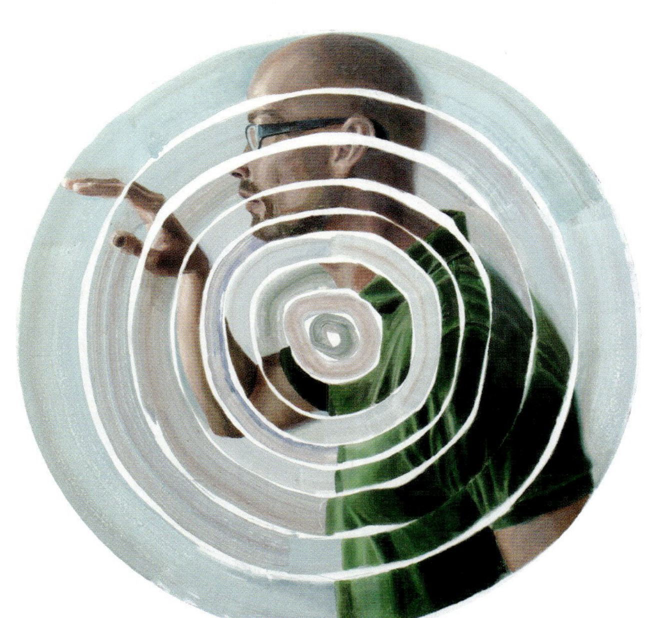

Seeing Is Believing
2014, ∅ 120 cm, oil on canvas

Glasglocke

Das Sichtbare scheint für Dénesh Ghyczy Ausgangspunkt einer Reise in das Innere der Seele. Auf vielen seiner Bilder haben die Porträtierten ihre Augen geschlossen. Sie hören nach innen. Sie suchen Kontakt zu etwas, das im Bild selbst als Dargestelltes nicht eindeutig sichtbar wird und wohl auch nicht sichtbar werden kann. Dennoch vernehmen wir diese Dimension, da es seinen Bildern gelingt, ein emphatisches Fenster auf den inneren Erfahrungsraum ihrer Bildprotagonisten zu öffnen. Im äußeren Eindruck seiner Malerei schwingt etwas vom Weltinnenraum seiner Protagonisten mit, sei es aus Einfühlung und Übertragung, aufgrund der bildnerischen Lösungen oder einer Mischung aus beidem. Ghyczy jedenfalls zeigt sich am Menschen als Erfahrungswesen interessiert, weshalb er mit seinen Bildern nicht selten metaphysische Grunderfahrungen wie das tiefgreifende Erleben des Getrenntseins oder den freien Fall ins Unbestimmte berührt. Und dann zeigen uns seine Darstellungen immer wieder intime Momenten der Begegnung mit sich selbst: als tastende Selbstvergewisserung oder in Erfahrungsformen körperlicher Entgrenzung und entfesselnder Befreiung.

Angesichts der bildlichen Auflösung der körperlichen Integrität auf vielen seiner Bilder lässt sich sogar die tückische Frage des Subjekts entfalten. Und sie ließe sich ebenso gut in psychologischer oder philosophischer wie auch in spiritueller Perspektive stellen. Ist das Ego nichts als eine Fata Morgana? Sind wir umgekehrt mehr, als wir von uns wissen und zu sehen glauben? Gibt es so etwas wie ein Kernsubjekt oder ist das beschworene Ich am Ende doch nur ein lose zusammengestückeltes Patchwork von Sinnesdaten, biografischen Erfahrungswerten und autogenen Selbsthypnosen ... die Ich-Bildung möglicherweise nur basierend auf der verlockenden, aber täuschenden Ganzheit

thing cannot actually become visible but he does succeed in making it perceptible because his paintings open up an empathic window to the inner experiential spaces of their protagonists. The external impression of his art carries with it something of the internal world of his protagonists. This may come from his empathy and transference, or from the artistic techniques chosen, or a blend of both.

In any case, it is obvious Ghyczy is interested in the person as a being that experiences, which is why his pictures often touch upon fundamental metaphysical experiences such as that of separation or of free fall into the unknown. And then his portrayals repeatedly reveal intimate moments of self-encounter: as tentative self-affirmation or as physical dissolution and unbinding liberation.

The dissolution of physical integrity depicted in many of his pictures allows us to tackle the tricky question of the subject, which can be and has been asked in psychological, philosophical, or spiritual terms. Is the ego nothing other than a fata morgana? Or are we actually more than we think we know and see of ourselves? Is there something like a core subject, or is the conspired ego or I actually just a loosely bound together patchwork of sensory data, biographical experiences, and autogenic self-hypnosis ... with the ego formation possibly basing itself merely on the seductive but deceptive entirety of a reflection in the mirror? Is it, in the end, only the imaginary unity of our physical self as we look in the mirror that keeps us bound within a “one” from an early age? [5]

Ghyczy’s early pictures in particular demonstrate effects that are not merely the optical effects of views broken up by glasses, panes, and lenses: the distorted or fragmented bodies also depict a pictorial anatomy of human self-exploration. They make visible how the ground sways beneath our feet or how we get caught in unavoidable illusions if we try to grasp our own self or the selves of others.

One Thought
2014, 160 x 130 cm, acrylic and oil on canvas

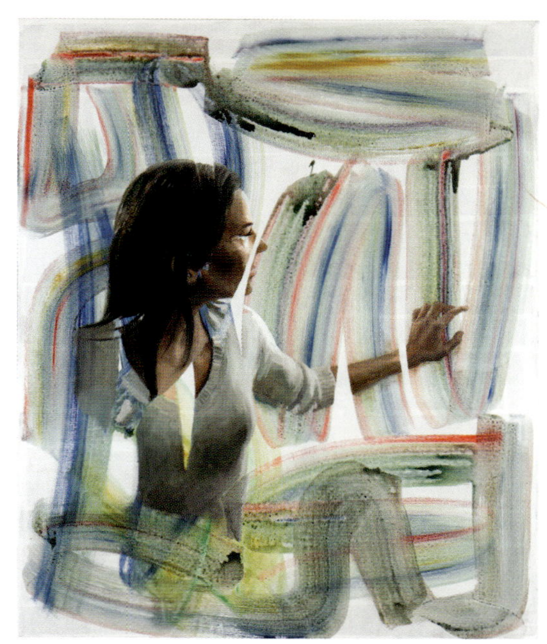

unseres Spiegelbildes. Ist es am Ende nur die imaginäre Einheit unseres körperlichen Selbst beim Blick in den Spiegel, die uns von Kindesbeinen an in eins bannt? [5]

Gerade seine frühen Bilder zeigen in den durch Gläser, Scheiben und Linsen gebrochenen Blicken nicht allein optische Effekte. Die verzerrten oder fragmentierten Körper bilden auch die bildliche Anatomie menschlicher Selbsterkundung ab. Sie lassen die schwankenden Gründe und unvermeidbaren Täuschungen beim Versuch, sich selbst oder andere zu erfassen, sichtbar werden.

Im Glas findet sich darüber hinaus auch eine unsichtbare Grenze formuliert, was besonders in jenen Bildern deutlich wird, auf denen die Hände der Dargestellten auf den transparenten Oberflächen entlangtasten. Glas ist nur für Blicke durchlässig, für alle anderen Sinne begrenzt es den Austausch und trennt zuletzt körperliche und soziale Welten. Wenn der Blick durch Glas auch eine distanzierte, geschützte und unbeteiligte Sicht auf die Dinge garantiert, so definiert es als Trennmedium zugleich eine undurchdringliche, kalte und wenigstens im metaphorischen Gebrauch auch psychosoziale Barriere.

Was bleibt von einem Menschen übrig, der in vollkommener Isolation lebt? Oder das Leben in beklemmender innerer Gefangenschaft erfährt? Was bedeutet es, durch eine unsichtbare gläserne Wand oder durch eine Glasglocke von der Welt abgeschnitten zu sein. In einer solchen gläsernen Optik haben beispielsweise Marlen Haushofer in ihrem Roman *Die Wand* [6] und Sylvia Plath in ihrem beklemmenden Lebensprotokoll *Glasglocke* [7] von den existenziellen Grunderfahrungen ihrer Protagonistinnen berichtet. Glas schützt, indem es abschirmt, während es zugleich ein unüberwindbares Hindernis bleibt: undurchlässig für alles Lebendige, vermag sich deshalb darin eine sinnbildliche Erfahrung innerer Emigration ausdrücken. In den Bildern von Dénesh

Additionally, by using glass the artist also formulates an invisible boundary. This becomes especially visible in the pictures where the figure's hands explore a transparent surface. Glass is only transparent to the sense of sight: for all other senses it blocks any exchange and can even separate physical and social worlds. If looking through glass can guarantee a distanced, protected, and impartial view of things, then as a medium of separation it must also define an impenetrable, cold, and, at least metaphorically, psychosocial barrier.

What is left over from a person who lives in complete social isolation? Or who experiences their life as taking place in an oppressive inner prison? What does it mean to be cut off from the world by an invisible glass wall or a bell jar? The existential experience within a glassy perception such as this characterizes the lives reported on by Marlen Haushofer in her novel *The Wall* [6] or Sylvia Plath in her harrowing, fictional novel about her life *The Bell* Jar [7]. Glass protects by putting a barrier around the protected, but in doing so it remains a barrier that cannot be overcome by the protected: it is impenetrable for every living thing, and can therefore serve as an allegory for the experience of an individual's alienation from the society he or she inhabits. In the pictures of Dénesh Ghyczy, this dimension is not depicted as a life-threatening experience of limits, such as in the two aforementioned books, but he nonetheless enables an experience of the separation caused by this transparent medium, building this into his systematic exploration of the visible world behind the glass.

The Small World of a Soap Bubble

In one early picture, *Good Idea,* 2003, a young woman can be seen who is playfully balancing some sort of soap bubble on her middle fin-

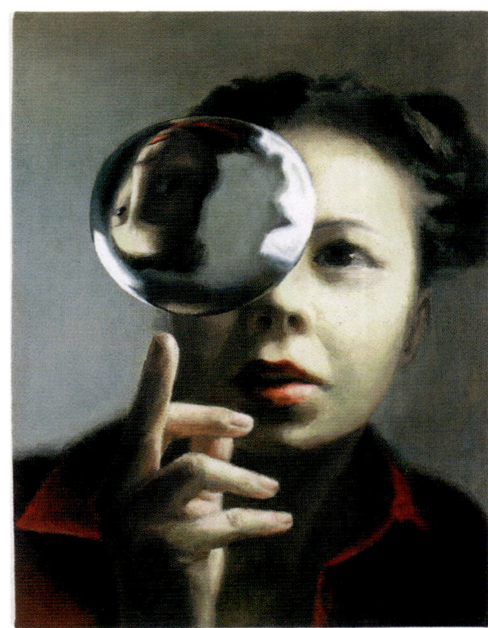

Good Idea
2003, 80 x 60 cm, acrylic on canvas

Ghyczy ist diese Dimension nicht als lebensbedrohende Grenzerfahrung vor Augen geführt, wie das in den beiden genannten Romanen der Fall ist, doch in die systematische Erkundung der sichtbaren Welt hinter den Gläsern ist doch auch bei ihm die Trennungserfahrung dieses transparenten Bildmediums eingelassen.

Kleine Welt der Seifenblase

Auf einem frühen Bild *Good Idea,* 2003, ist eine junge Frau zu beobachten, wie sie spielerisch eine Art Seifenblase auf ihrem Mittelfinger jongliert. Gebannt wie ein kleines Kind, liegt ihre ganze Aufmerksamkeit in der Betrachtung jener faszinierenden Spiegelung, die das verzerrte Abbild der eigenen Gesichtszüge auf der Kugeloberfläche einfängt. Bildgeschichtlich erscheint dieses Bild wie eine Mischung aus dem berühmten Selbstbildnis in einem konvexen Spiegel von Parmigianino [8] und einem vergleichsweise unbekannten Seifenblasenbild von Sir John Everett Millais, [9] das allerdings Peter Sloterdijk zu seiner Einleitung in die *Sphären*-Trilogie inspirierte. [10]

Das beschriebene Bild hält den schwebenden Moment fest, in dem die Aufmerksamkeit aus dem Körper tritt, um diesen im Äußeren ansichtig zu werden. Aus der Faszination für die spiegelnde Oberfläche wird plötzlich ein Medium der Selbstbetrachtung. Dass damit zugleich auch die Gefährdung einer veritablen Täuschung mitschwingt, davon zeugt eine verwandte mythische Urszene tragischer Selbstverkennung: Narziss ist es, der sich beim Blick in eine Quelle unsterblich in sein eigenes Spiegelbild verliebt – nicht zuletzt auch deshalb, weil er sich zunächst nicht selbst darin erkennt. Auf dem Bild *Your Intention,* 2014, zeigt uns Dénesh Ghyczy die seitliche Profilansicht einer blonden Frau, deren Gesicht ihr auf der rechten Bildhälfte als wellenhaft bewegte Spiegelung

ger. Like a small child, spellbound, her full attention is focused on the fascinating reflections on the surface of the bubble, showing a distorted image of her own face. In terms of art history, this picture appears as a mixture of the famous *Self-portrait in a Convex Mirror* by Parmigianino [8] and a comparatively unknown soap-bubble painting by Sir John Everett Millais, [9] which inspired Peter Sloterdijk in writing his introduction to the *Spheres* trilogy. [10]

Ghyczy's painting captures the transitory moment when our attention leaves our body in order to enable our external perception of it. Suddenly, a medium of self-reflection develops out of the fascination for external surface reflections. However, a related mythical scene depicting ancient self-deception reminds us there is a risk of illusion inherent in this: Narcissus is the one who falls undyingly in love with his own reflection as he looks into a pool. Not least because he initially does not actually recognize himself. In his later painting *Your Intention,* 2014, Dénesh Ghyczy shows us the profile of a blonde woman encountering her own face in a wave-like reflection across the right side of the picture. She appears curious and sufficiently willing to take a much closer look at this fluid matrix. She is purposefully approaching her reflection, in the same way we would press our nose against a pane of glass, to get a better look and find out what this mirror is all about, or what impenetrable dimensions might be hidden behind it. The profile of the young woman appears to be a visual echo of the character in the ancient myth.

Common to both of these pictures is a person confronting themselves in an external medium of self-observation. Whereas the first one mainly links a person's playful interest in their own image with a fascination for the external world, the figure in the latter painting has a will that penetrates the medium: a desire to attain self-knowledge. Maybe the

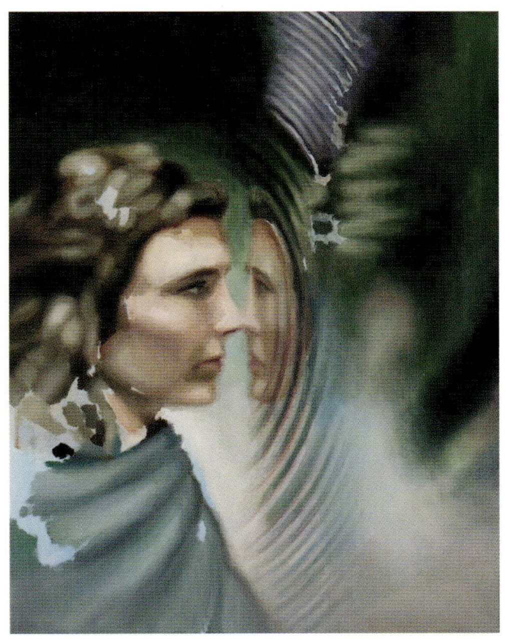

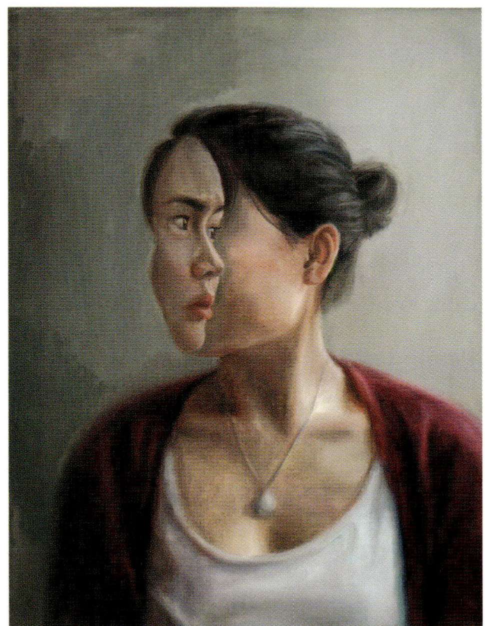

Your Intention
2014, 80 x 60 cm, oil on canvas, (left)

Insight
2014, 80 x 60 cm, oil on canvas (right)

entgegenschlägt. Sie scheint neugierig und gewillt genug, dieser fluiden Matrix entschieden auf den Grund zu gehen. Bestimmt nähert sie sich ihrem Spiegelbild, wie man sich die Nase an einer Scheibe platt drückt, wohl um besser sehen zu können, was es mit dieser Spiegelung auf sich hat oder welche undurchschaubare Dimension sich dahinter verbergen könnte. Die Profilansicht der jungen Frau wirkt wie ein bildliches Echo auf die mythische Männergestalt.

Beiden Bildern ist gemein, dass die Personen sich in einem äußeren Medium der Selbstbetrachtung begegnen. Während in Ersterem vor allem das spielerische Interesse am eigenen Bild mit der Faszination für die äußere Welt verbunden wurde, lässt Letzteres einen das Medium durchdringenden Willen zur Selbsterkenntnis aufscheinen. Vielleicht wäre die junge Frau sogar gewillt, durch diese Schicht der Spiegelung auf die andere Seite zu gelangen. Dorthin, wo die Körper möglicherweise keine Schatten besitzen und das Ich kein Gesicht kennt. [11]

Hinter die Schleier der Selbsttäuschung zu gelangen – und damit befassen sich diese Bilder –, ist ein wesentlicher Aspekt der spirituellen Übung. In vielen Bildern, besonders jenen der Serie *Silent Mantras,* spielen bei Ghyczy die Erfahrungen der Meditation eine bedeutende Rolle. Anders als in den genannten Beispiele schlägt das Gemälde *Insight,* 2014, den entgegengesetzten Weg einer verinnerlichenden Selbstbetrachtung ein, der im Titel schon anklingt. In einer Picasso paraphrasierenden Bildwendung ist hier ein Teil des Frauengesichts aus seinem Umriss gelöst und nach innen gestülpt. Das Ich wendet sich von der äußeren Welt ab, um Einsicht in das eigene Sein zu gewinnen und der Natur des Bewusstseins zu begegnen. Für diesen Vorgang, der zugleich den Beginn jeder Meditation bezeichnet, findet Ghyczy hier die bildliche Formulierung einer nach innen gewendeten Interfazialität. Zwar findet sich das Gesicht als Einheit und damit auch als biomorphi-

young woman would even have wanted to break through this layer of reflection to reach the other side. A realm where the body might cast no shadows and the ego might have no face. [11]

Gaining access to the world behind the veil of self-deception—that is, after all, the subject of these pictures—is a significant aspect of spiritual practice. In many pictures, especially those in the series *Silent Mantras*, meditation experiences play an important role for Ghyczy. In contrast to the prior examples, the painting *Insight,* 2014, takes another path: an internalizing self-reflection (as the title already suggests). In a recasting of the image that paraphrases Picasso, part of the female face is lifted out, turned around, and re-inserted into the face's outline. The figure's ego is turning away from the external world in order to gain insight into her own being and encounter the nature of consciousness. For this process, which also characterizes the start of any meditation, Ghyczy finds a way for his picture to express an inward-looking interfaciality. Although the face gives up its unity and role as biomorphic information carrier for the person, the ego does nonetheless form recognizably within the stable outline of this facial field, as a minimal communion. [12]

The Bound Soul and the Liberation of Painting

As seeker, falling body, bound soul, or in oblivious action: it is the figure of the solitary individual that almost always forms the focus of Dénesh Ghyczy's paintings.

The path his paintings take leads us from the naturalistic reproduction of what is visible to the senses to a more free unfolding of graphic powers and pictorial processes. Initially, even his photo-realistic distortion stuck closely to its optical conditions. Later, his artistic development moved between the poles of abstraction and objectivity, at times

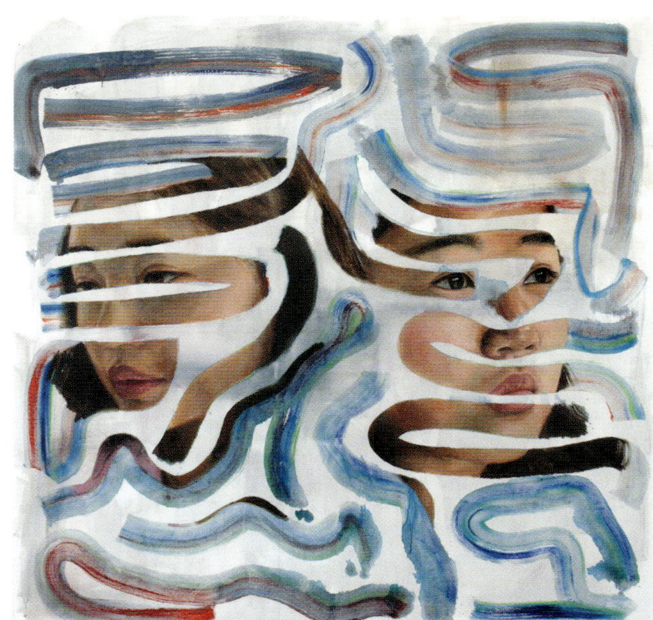

Two Faces of Momo
2014, 200 x 200 cm, acrylic and oil on canvas

scher Informationsträger der Person aufgegeben, dafür aber formiert sich in dem dennoch stabilen Umriss dieses Gesichtsfeldes das Ich als minimale Kommune. [12]

Die gefesselte Seele und die Befreiung der Malerei

Als Suchender, als Fallender, als gefesselte Seele oder in selbstvergessenem Tun: Im Blickpunkt der Bilder von Dénesh Ghyczy erscheint fast immer die Figur eines einzelnen Menschen.

Der Weg seiner Malerei führte dabei von der naturgetreuen Wiedergabe des sinnlich Sichtbaren zu einer freieren Entfaltung der bildnerischen Kräfte und malerischen Prozesse. Anfangs blieb selbst die fotorealistische Verzerrung meist eng an ihre optischen Bedingungen gebunden. Später kreiste seine Entwicklung dann zwischen den Polen von Abstraktion und Gegenständlichkeit, pendelte manchmal hin und her oder führte vor und wieder zurück. Zuletzt befreite Ghyczy sich zunehmend von der alleinigen Verpflichtung auf die Wahrheit des Gesehenen, ohne sich allerdings von der figürlichen Darstellung im Ganzen abzuwenden. Im Gegenteil: Seine jüngeren Bilder leben vom vitalen Kontrast figürlicher Elemente mit abstrakten Kräften. Wie auch die Figuren auf manchen seiner Bilder entfesselt auftreten, scheint die Befreiung von zu eng bestimmten bildlichen Konventionen neue malerische und bildliche Energien freizusetzen.

Bei einer ganzen Reihe seiner jüngsten Bilder sind Fessel und Befreiung wiederkehrende Motive. Sowohl Männer als auch Frauen sind dort in unterschiedlichen Positionen gefesselt dargestellt. In einigen Fällen löst sich die Fessel. Manchmal laufen auch Streifen und Farbbahnen wie sinnbildliche Supplemente gelöster Fesseln durch die Bilder und die dargestellten Figuren hindurch. Oder wild auffliegende Haare bilden

swinging more quickly back and forth and at times leading more firmly in one direction before turning back. Then, in his latest phase, Ghyczy has liberated himself from any sole obligation to the truth of the visible, although he never completely moved away from figurative portrayal. Quite the opposite: his recent pictures gain their vitality from the contrast between figurative elements and abstract powers. In the same way as the figures in some of his paintings appear unbound, the liberation of over-controlled artistic conventions has set free new energies with regard to both the image itself and the painting techniques used.

In a whole series of his most recent paintings, bondage and liberation serve as motifs. Both men and women are portrayed in a variety of positions—but bound. In some cases the bindings are coming loose. Sometimes stripes and swathes of color run through the paintings and their figures like symbolic supplements of untied bindings. Or, in *Two Faces of Momo,* 2014, and *Wandering Mind,* 2014, wildly thrashing hair and brushstrokes snaking their way across the painting combine to form a liberatingly expressive gesture, whose unbinding playfully turns into dancing elements choreographing the picture. [13]
Obviously these more recent pictures also hint at the erotic practices of bondage, but as with Michelangelo's monumental *slaves* they can be read in a much more general way as an allegory of unliberated human nature and an expression of how the soul is bound to the mortal body despite its deep longing to be free.

In these images, Dénesh Ghyczy plays through situations where his figures are being moved by both binding energies and liberating powers. As in the paintings where people are falling or dropping, here we also find him making a theme out of the psychology of letting go and trust: where surrender liberates his subject from their profane decision-making responsibilities. Bondage and liberation complement

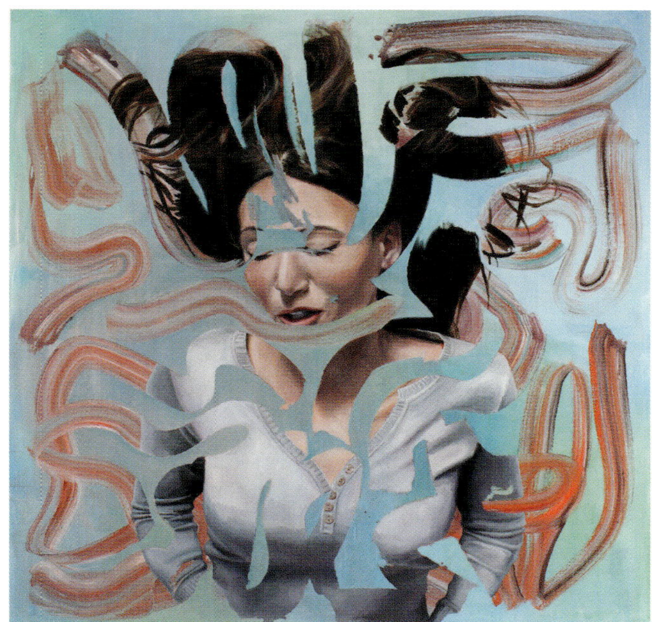

Wandering Mind
2015, 190 x 190 cm, acrylic and oil on canvas

im Einklang mit den sich über die Bildfläche schlängelnden Pinselbahnen *Two Faces of Momo,* 2014, und *Wandering Mind,* 2014, eine befreiend expressive Geste, deren Entfesselung spielerisch in tänzerische und bildchoreografische Elemente übergeht. [13]

Offensichtlich spielen diese neueren Bilder zwar auf erotische Praktiken des Bondage an, sie lassen sich aber wie einst schon die monumentalen *Sklaven* Michelangelos in einem weitaus allgemeineren Sinn als Allegorie der unfreien menschlichen Natur, als Ausdruck der Fesselung der Seele im endlichen Körper und ihrer tiefen Sehnsucht nach Befreiung lesen.

Dénesh Ghyczy spielt in diesen Bildern Situationen durch, in denen seine Figuren von Bindungsenergien und Entfesselungskräften bewegt werden. Wie schon in den Bildern mit fallenden oder stürzenden Menschen findet sich auch hier eine Psychologie des Loslassens und Vertrauens thematisiert, die das Subjekt in hingebungsvoller Selbstaufgabe von seiner profanen Entscheidungsverantwortung befreit. Fessel und Befreiung ergänzen sich, sie gehören zusammen, ja die Fessel selbst kann zum Instrument der Befreiung werden, wie auch der Körper zum Medium energetischer Entfesselung und seelischer Befreiung genutzt werden kann.

Im Tanz. Im Fallen. In der Entfesselung der Malerei. Denn auch sie, die Malerei, ist ein körperlicher Prozess – und die Fesselung der Sinne eine magische Aufgabe der Kunst.

Das Schwierigste ist zu sehen, was vor den Augen liegt. Doch mit einem Auge zu viel, wer weiß. Im entfesselten Körper der Malerei, so ließe sich schließen, emanzipiert sich das Medium vom Bild.

Wie viele Gesichter das Gegenüber, wie viele Augen der Betrachter auch hat. Wohin immer die Seele entkommt.

each other and belong together: yes, bindings can even become an instrument of liberation, just as our body can be used as a medium for the energetic unbinding and liberation of our soul.

In dance. In falling. In the unbinding nature of painting. After all, even the latter—painting as an art form—is a physical process. And the (un)binding of the senses is art's magical task.

Seeing what is in front of our eyes is one of the most difficult things we can do. But with an eye too many, who knows what becomes possible? In the liberated world of painting, so we can conclude, the medium is released from the image.

However many eyes may look at however many faces, wherever the emancipated soul may be.

[1] In manchem erinnert dieses Vorgehen und das malerische Ergebnis an die Bilder des amerikanischen Malers Chuck Close, der das primär Sichtbare in ein komplexes Bildfeld kleinteiliger, farbiger Abstraktionen auflöst. Beispiele sind zu finden etwa in: Chuck Close, *Retrospektive,* hrsg. v. Jochen Poetter u. Helmut Friedel, Austellungskatalog Baden- Baden 1994.

[2] Die Fotografie ist auf diesen Bilden ein technisches ‚a priori' des visuellen Effekts. Das Nacheinander der Bilder, wie sie in der frühen Chronofotografie bei Eadweard Muybridge u. a. zur Verblüffung des damaligen Augenscheins als Abfolge von Momentaufnahmen festgehalten wurde, wird hier in die Simultanität eines gemeinsamen Bildraumes eingelassen.

[3] Vgl. Honoré Balzac, *Das unbekannte Meisterwerk*, aus dem Französischen von Herma Goeppert-Frank, Berlin 1987. Hierzu auch Hans Belting, *Das unsichtbare Meisterwerk. Die modernen Mythen der Kunst,* München 1998.

[4] Vgl. dazu grundlegend: Jacques Derrida, *Aufzeichnungen eines Blinden. Das Selbstporträt und andere Ruinen,* München 1997.

[5] Vgl. Jacques Lacan, „Das Spiegelstadium als Bildner der Ichfunktion, wie sie uns in der psychoanalytischen Erfahrung erscheint (1948)", in: Ders, *Schriften I,* Weinheim/Berlin 1986, S. 61–70.

[6] Marlen Haushofer, *Die Wand,* Berlin 2004. Sehenswert mit Martina Gedeck in der Hauptrolle verfilmt: Regie u. Drehbuch von Julian Pölsler, Österreich/Deutschland 2012.

[7] Sylvia Plath, *Die Glasglocke,* Frankfurt am Main 1997.

[8] Parmigianino, *Selbstporträt im konvexen Spiegel*, 1523/24, Öl auf Pappelholz, Kunsthistorisches Museum, Wien.

[9] Sir John Everett Millais, *A Child's World,* 1886, Öl auf Leinwand, Lady Lever Art Gallery, Port Sunlight Village (Liverpool).

[1] In some ways this process and the resulting painting are reminiscent of the pictures of the American painter Chuck Close, who broke down what was initially visible into a complex picture of small, colorful, abstracted details. Examples can be found in: *Chuck Close, Retrospektive,* eds. Jochen Poetter and Helmut Friedel, exh. cat. Kunsthalle Baden-Baden (Ostfildern: Hatje Cantz, 1994).

[2] In these pictures, photography is a technical a *priori* for the visual effects. Whereas early chronophotography, such as that of Eadweard Muybridge, used the successionality of images to deceive and amaze the contemporary viewer, here the observer is offered entry into the simultaneity of a common image-space.

[3] See Honore Balzac, *The Unknown Masterpiece* (New York: Dover Publications, 2011). See also Hans Belting, *Das unsichtbare Meisterwerk. Die modernen Mythen der Kunst* (Munich: C.H. Beck, 2001).

[4] On this, see Jacques Derrida, *Memoirs of the Blind: The Self-Portrait and Other Ruins* (Chicago: University of Chicago Press, 1993).

[5] See Jacques Lacan, "The Mirror Stage as Formative of the Function of the I as Revealed in Psychoanalytic Experience," in *Ecrits, A Selection,* trans. Alan Sheridan (London: Tavistock Publications, 1977) pp. 502-509.

[6] Marlen Haushofer, *The Wall* (Berkeley: Cleis Press, 2004). Also worthy of recommendation is the film of the book, with Martina Gedeck in the main role: directed and written by Julian Pölsler, Austria-Germany, 2012.

[7] Sylvia Plath, *The Bell Jar* (New York: Harper Perennial, 2013).

[8] Parmigianino, *Self-Portrait in a Convex Mirror,* ca. 1524, oil on poplar, Kunsthistorisches Museum, Vienna.

[10] Peter Sloterdijk, *Sphären I, Blasen*, „Einleitung, Die Alliierten oder die gehauchte Kommune", Frankfurt am Main 1998, S. 17–82.

[11] Spiegel sind Eintrittsmotive in eine andere Welt wie in der berühmten Szene in Jean Cocteaus Film *Orphée*, Frankreich 1950.

[12] Zur Ideen- und Bildgeschichte der Interfazialität vgl. Sloterdijk 1998 (wie Anm. 10).

[13] Zugleich lassen diese Bilder unwillkürlich an das Medusenhaupt denken, womit ein weiteres Kapitel mythischer Erzählung aufzuschlagen wäre, in dem Blick und Bann, Lebendigkeit und Versteinerung eine zentrale Rolle spielen.

[9] Sir John Everett Millais, *A Child's World,* 1886, oil on canvas, Lady Lever Art Gallery, Port Sunlight Village (Liverpool).

[10] Peter Sloterdijk, *Spheres Volume I: Microspherology. Bubbles* (Cambridge: MIT Press, 2011).

[11] Mirrors are a common motif for entering another world, as in the famous scene by Jean Cocteau: *Orphée,* France 1950.

[12] On the history of the ideas and images of interfaciality, see Sloterdijk (2011)

[13] At the same time, these images involuntarily remind us of Medusa's head, which would open up another chapter of mystical tales in which a glance and a spell, vitality and petrification play a central role.

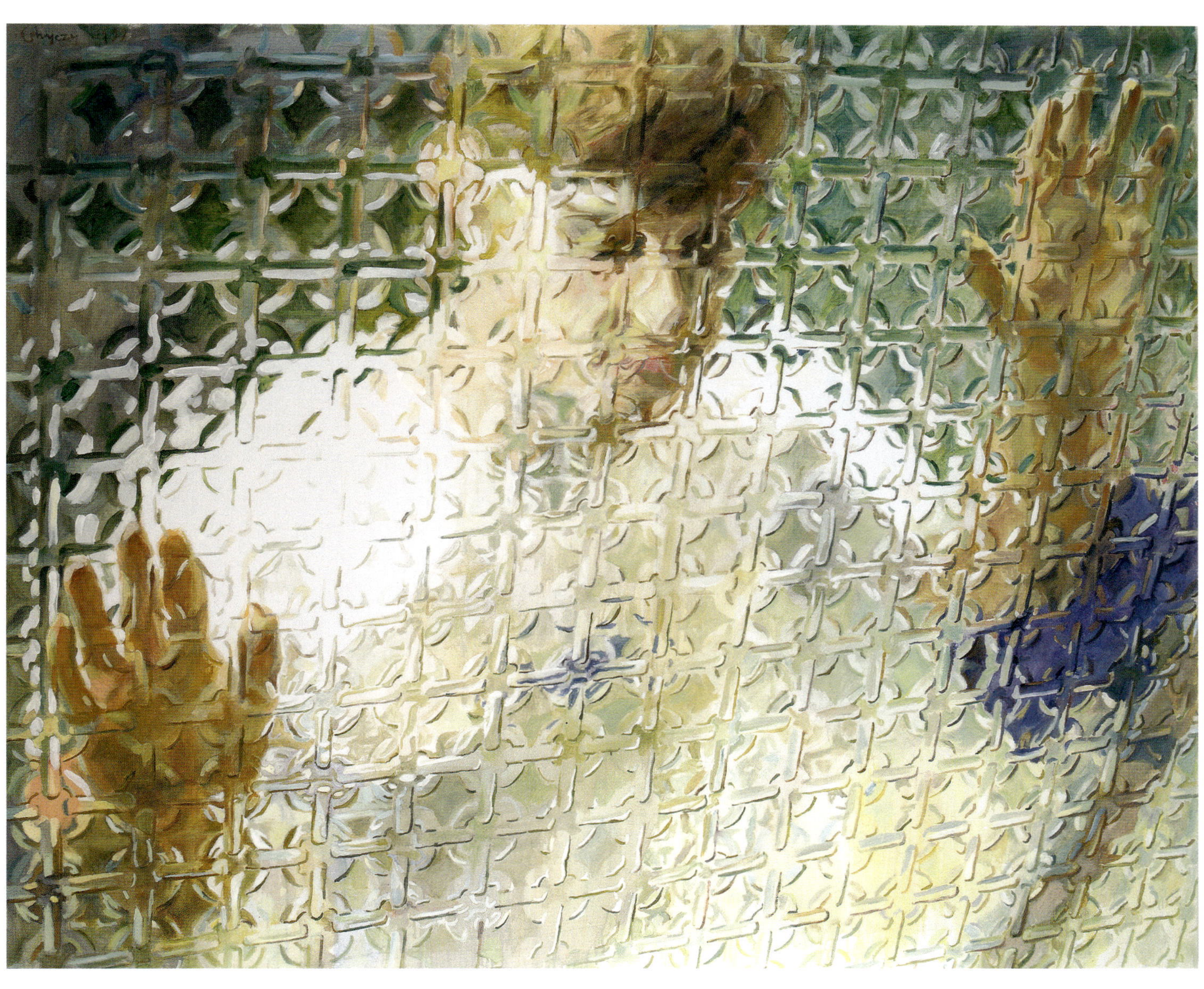

From Inside 1999, 155 x 190 cm, oil on canvas, private collection, London

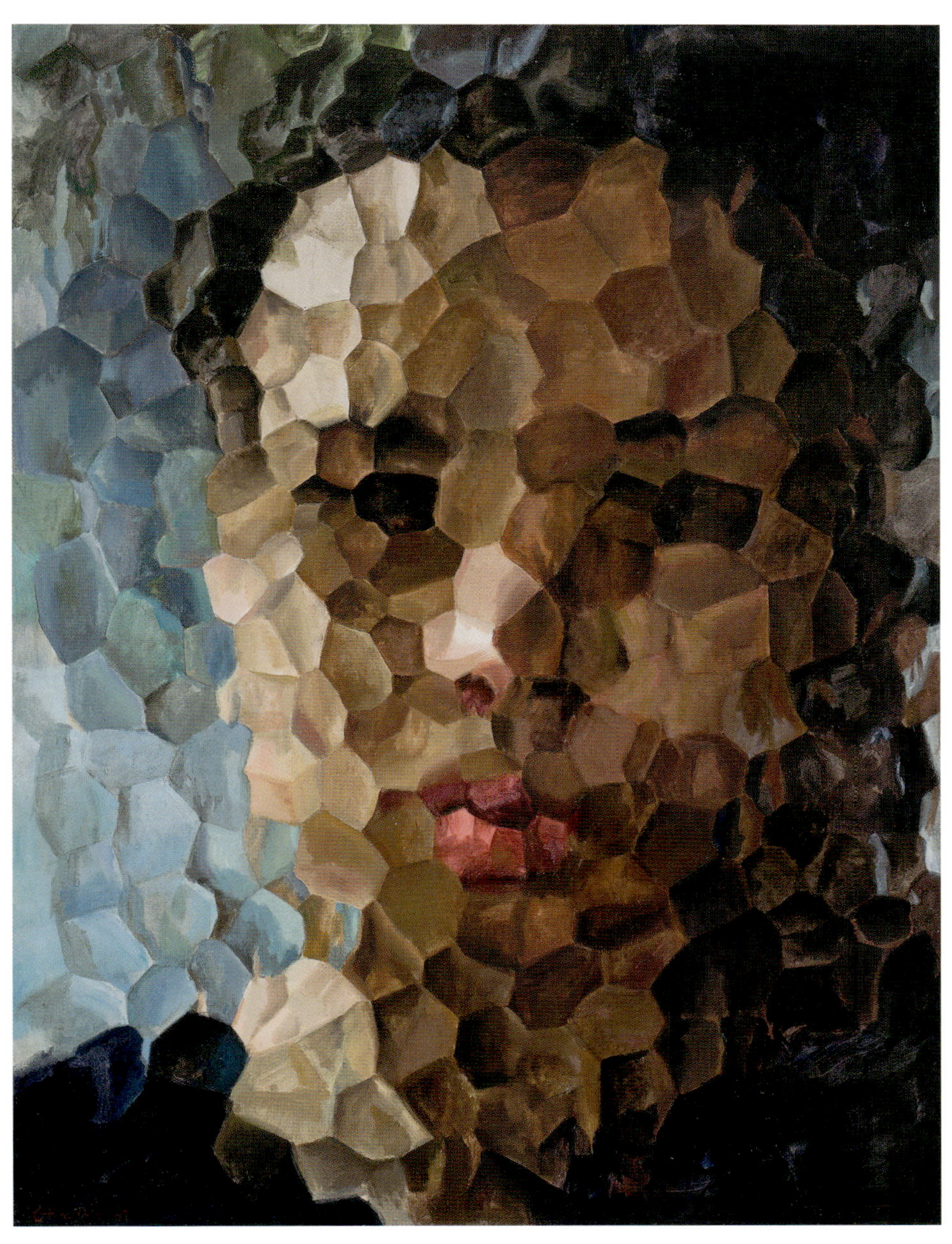

Mask 2001, 140 x 105 cm, acrylic on canvas

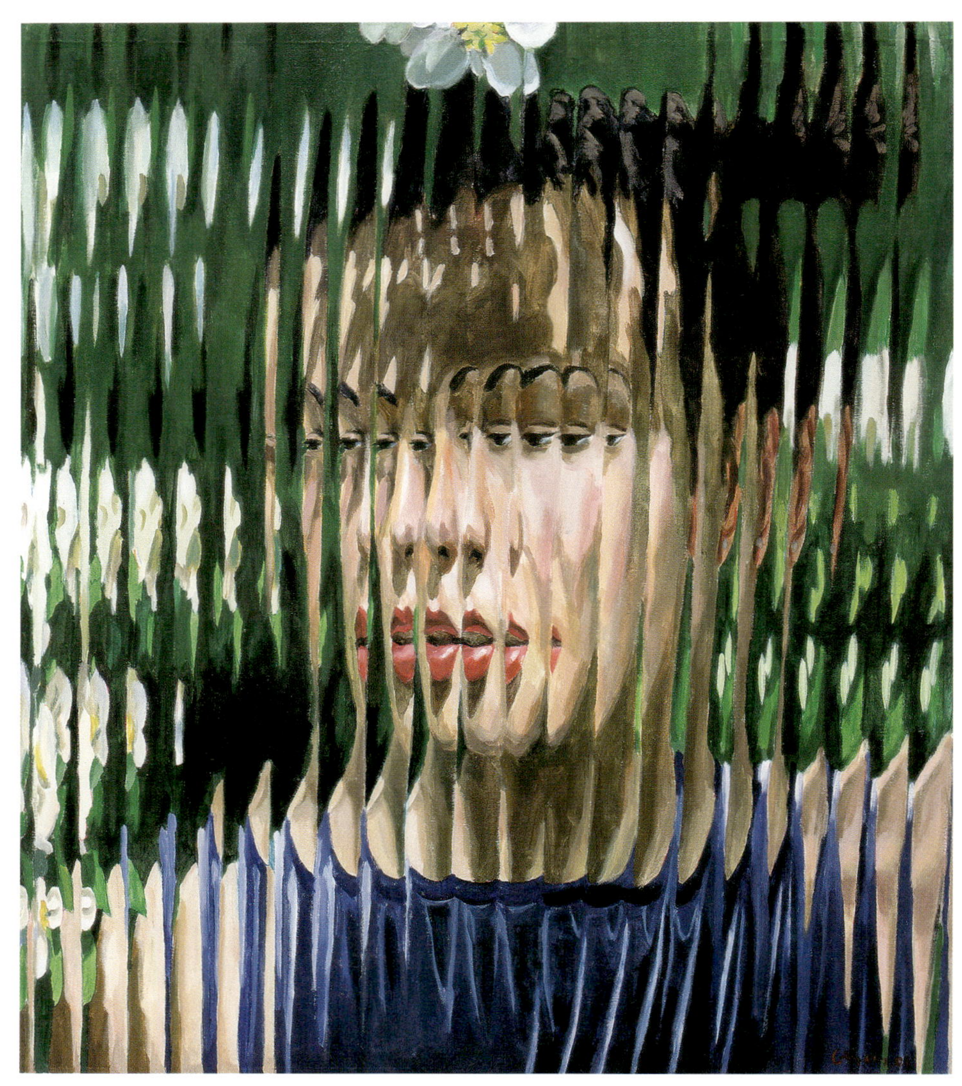

Glass Garden 2001, 128 x 110 cm, acrylic on canvas, private collection, Budapest

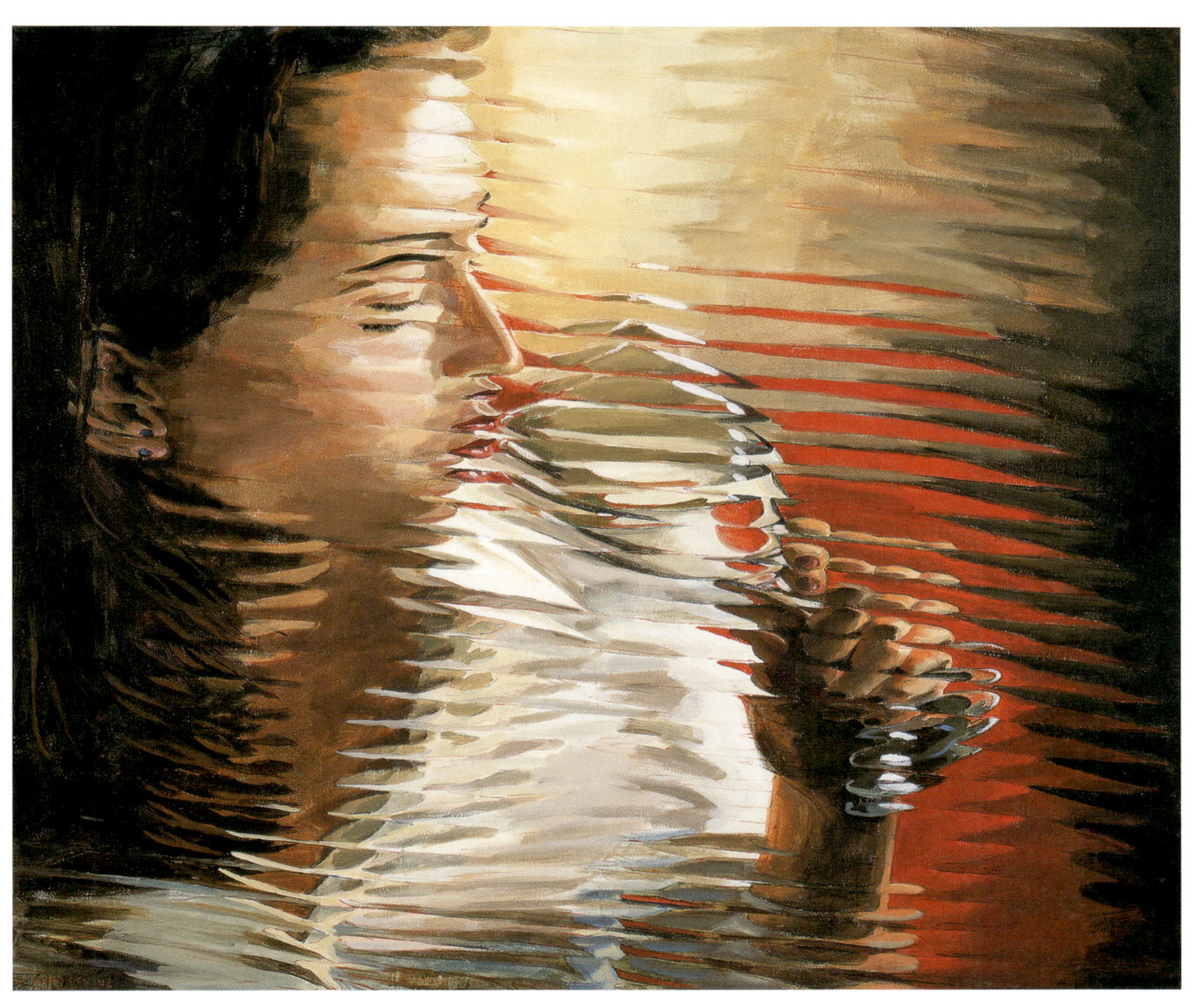

Fragile 2002, 120 x 140 cm, acrylic on canvas, private collection, Budapest

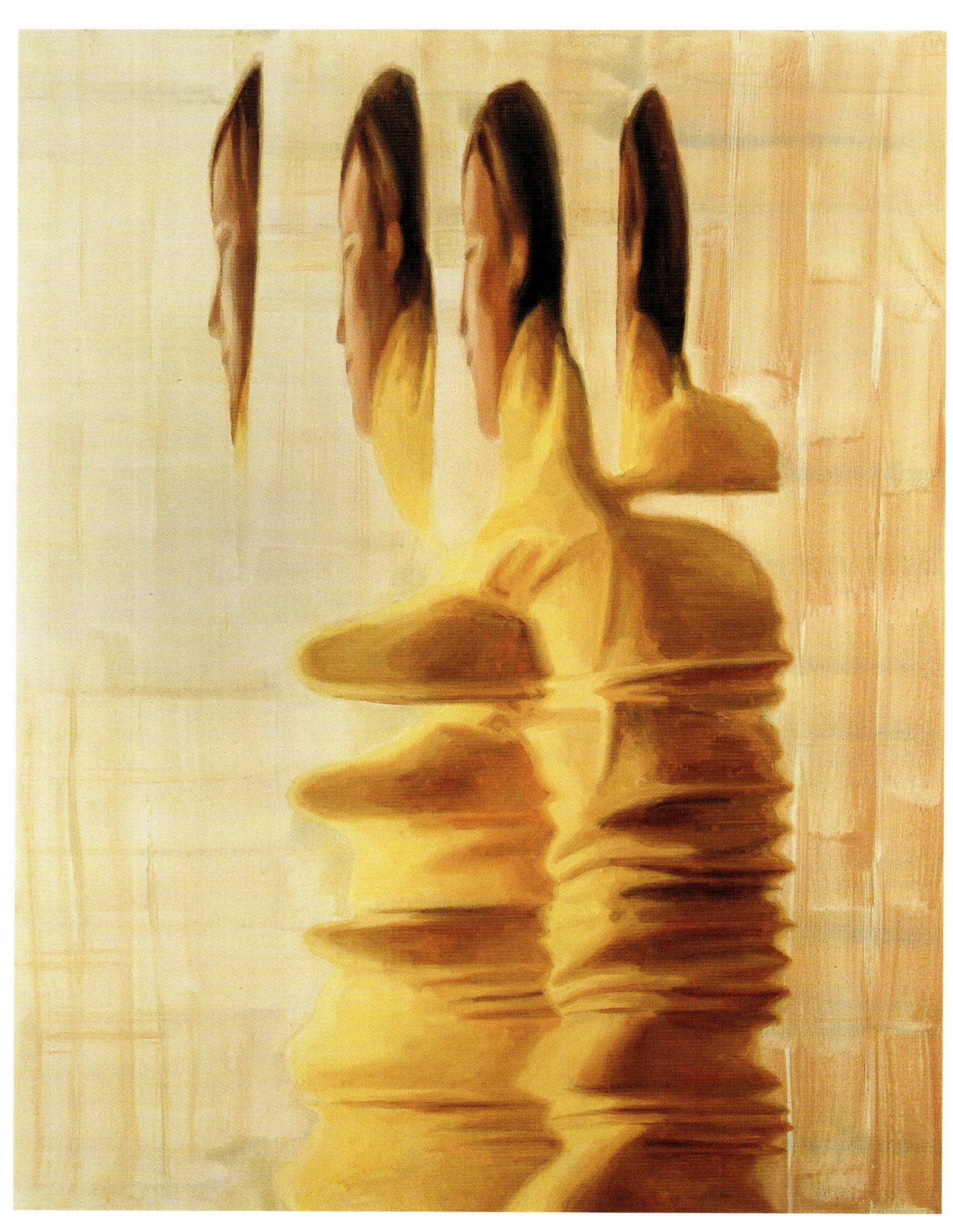

Yellow Turtle Neck 2006, 170 x 130 cm, oil and acrylic on canvas

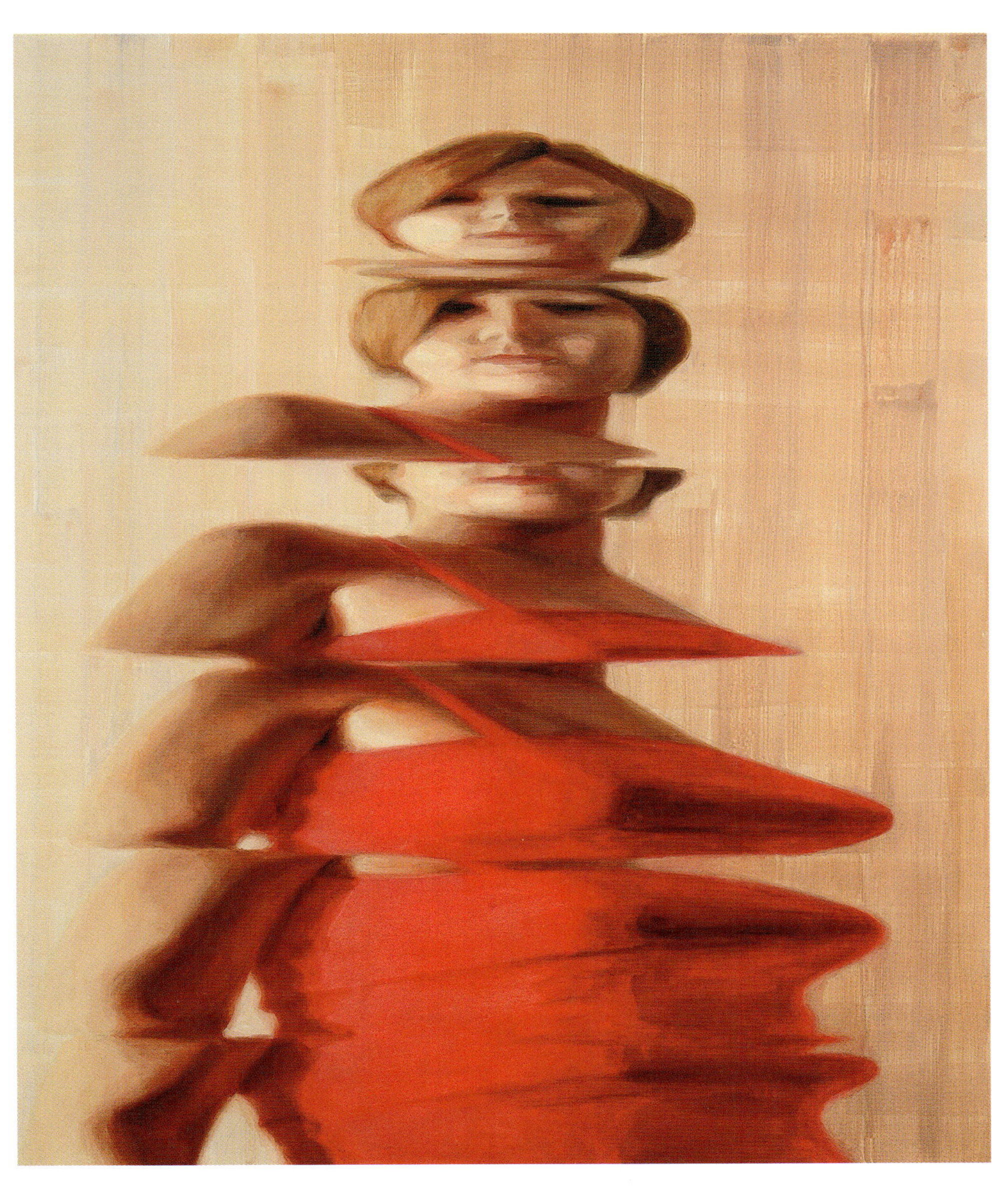

Rita 2006, 155 x 130 cm, oil and acrylic on canvas, private collection, Berlin

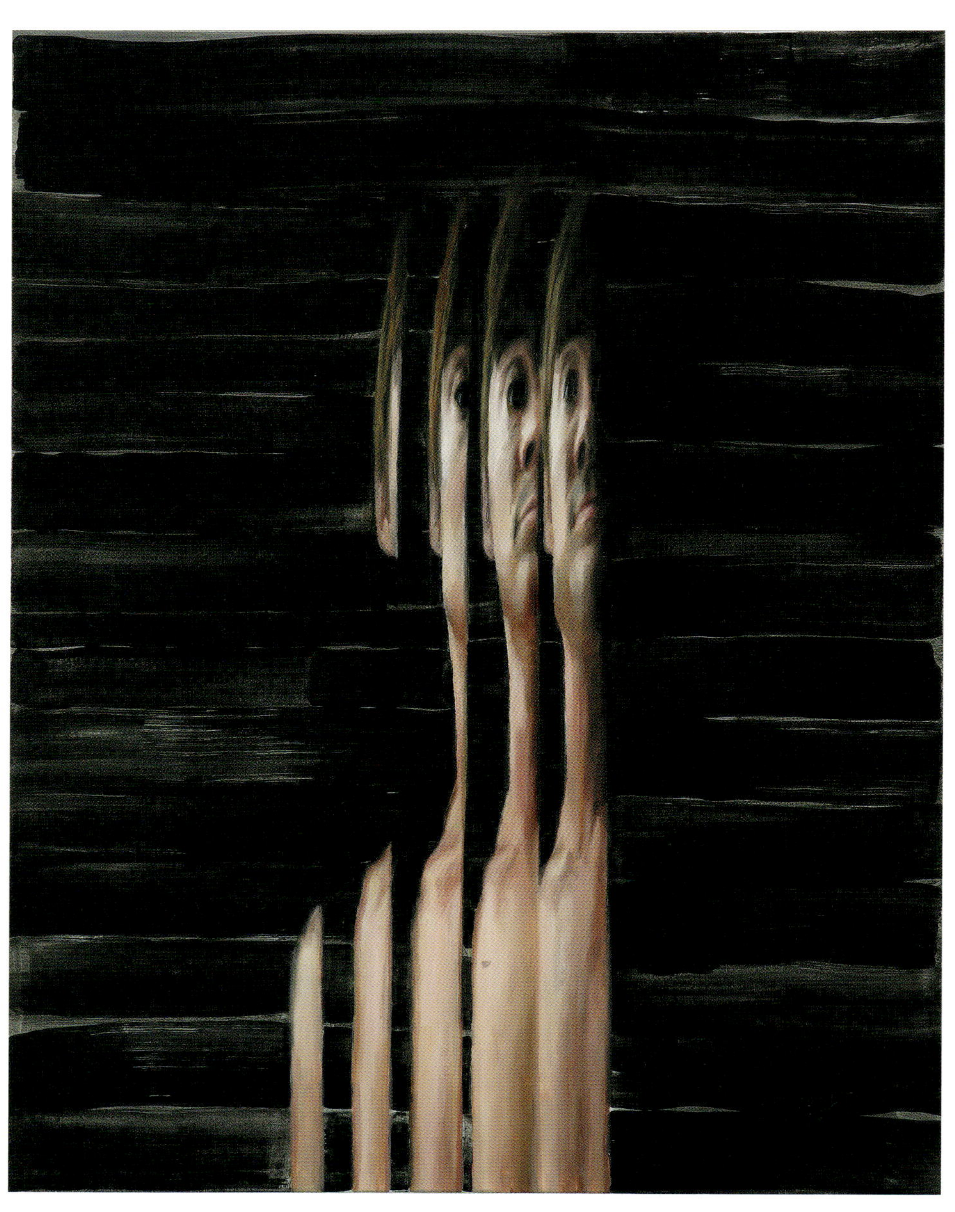

Felix 2006, 140 x 110 cm, oil and acrylic on canvas

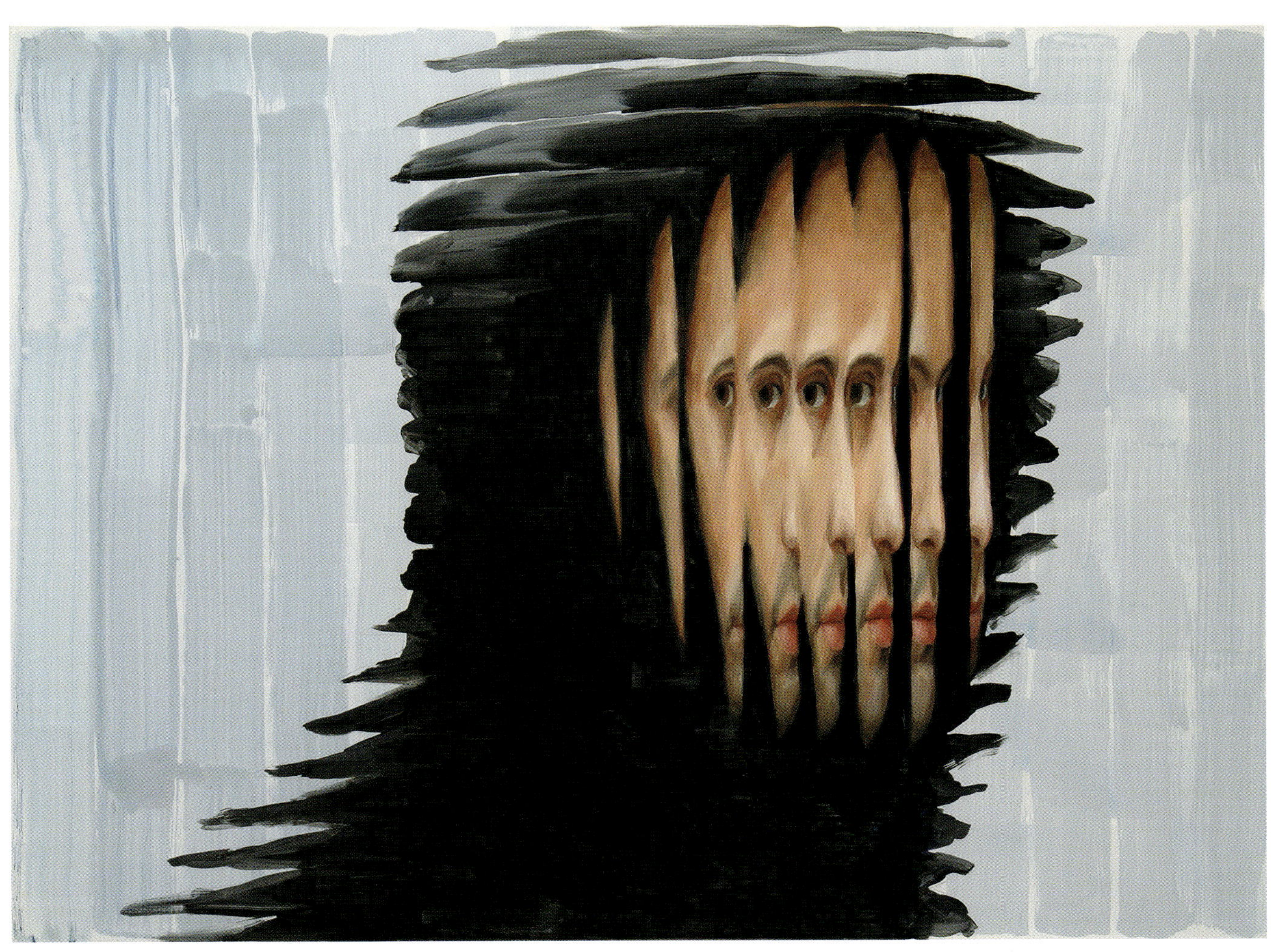

Kilian 2006, 120 x 160 cm, oil and acrylic on canvas

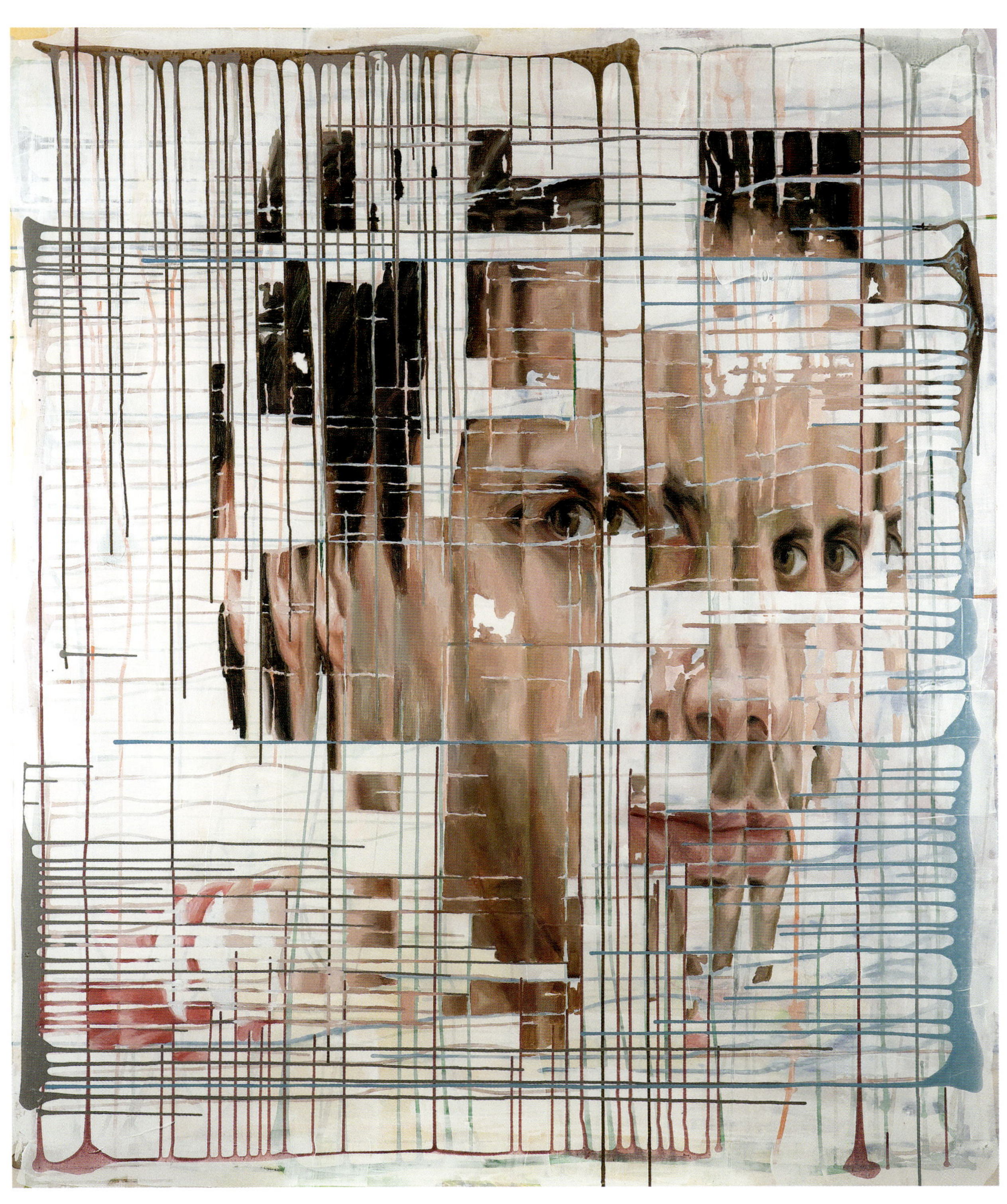

Kilian 2008, 170 x 140 cm, oil and acrylic on silk, private collection, Copenhagen

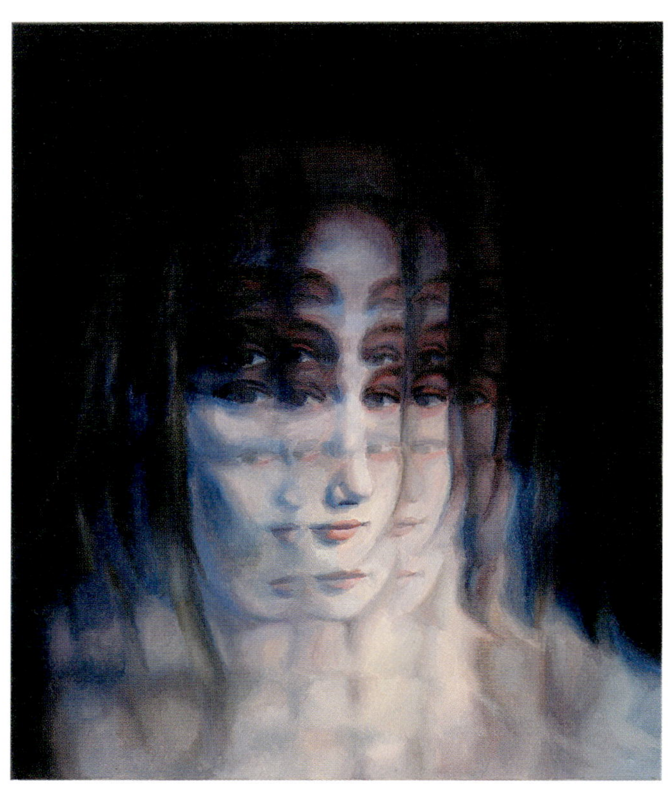

Sarah 2013, 60 x 50 cm, oil on canvas

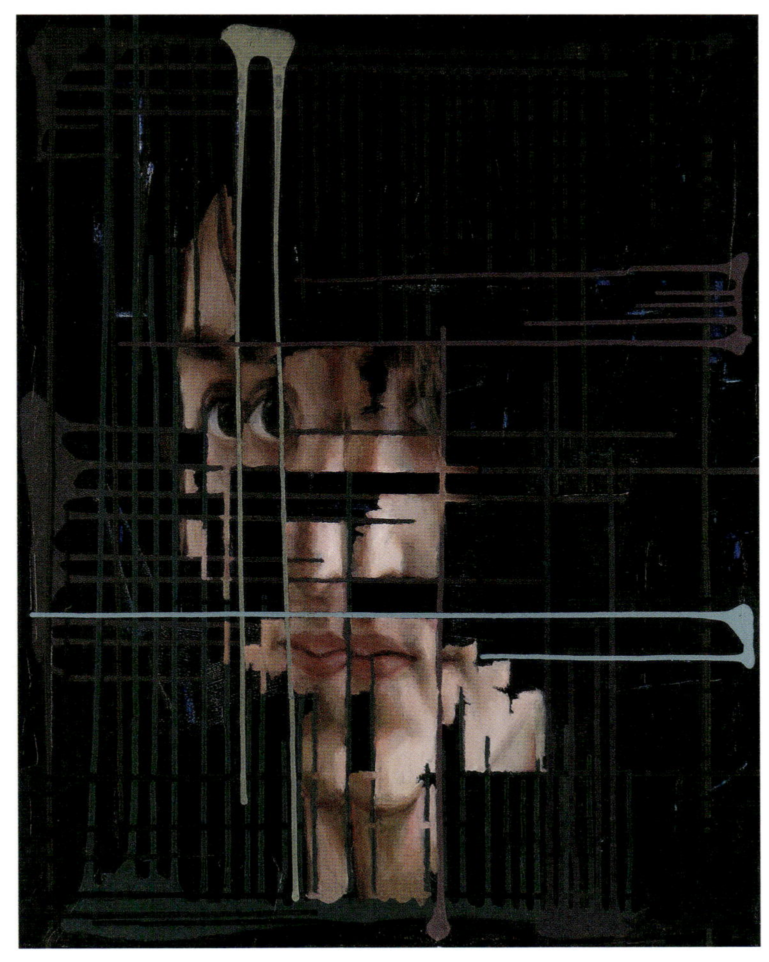

Nick 2008, 90 x 70 cm, oil and acrylic on canvas,
private collection, Copenhagen

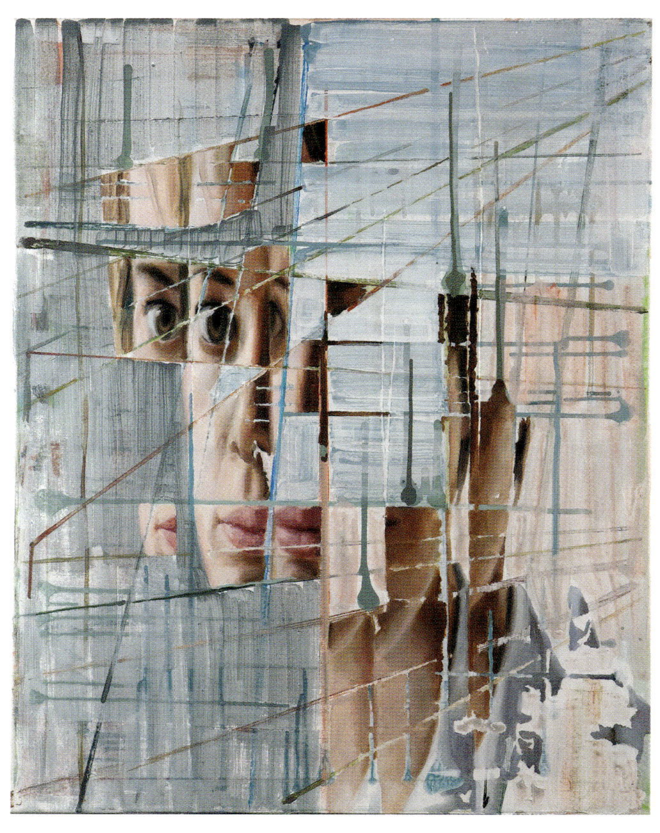

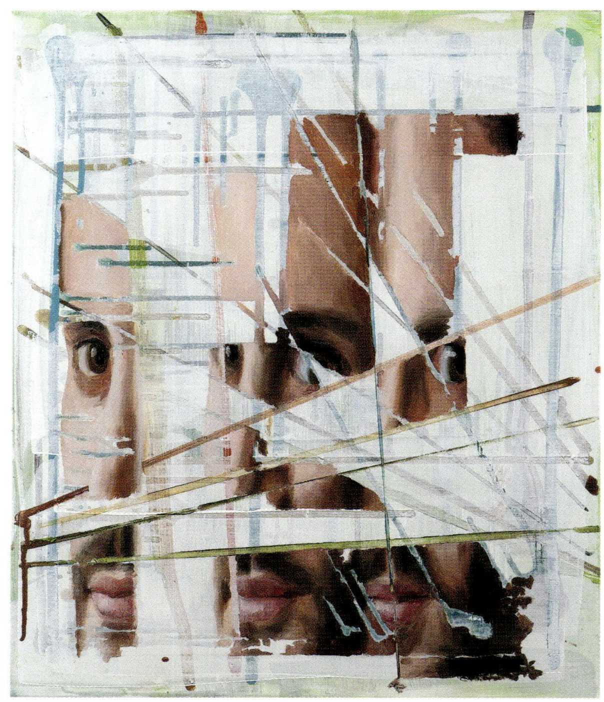

Rilana 2008, 90 x 70 cm, oil and acrylic on canvas, private collection, Berlin

Philip 2008, 60 x 50 cm, oil and acrylic on canvas

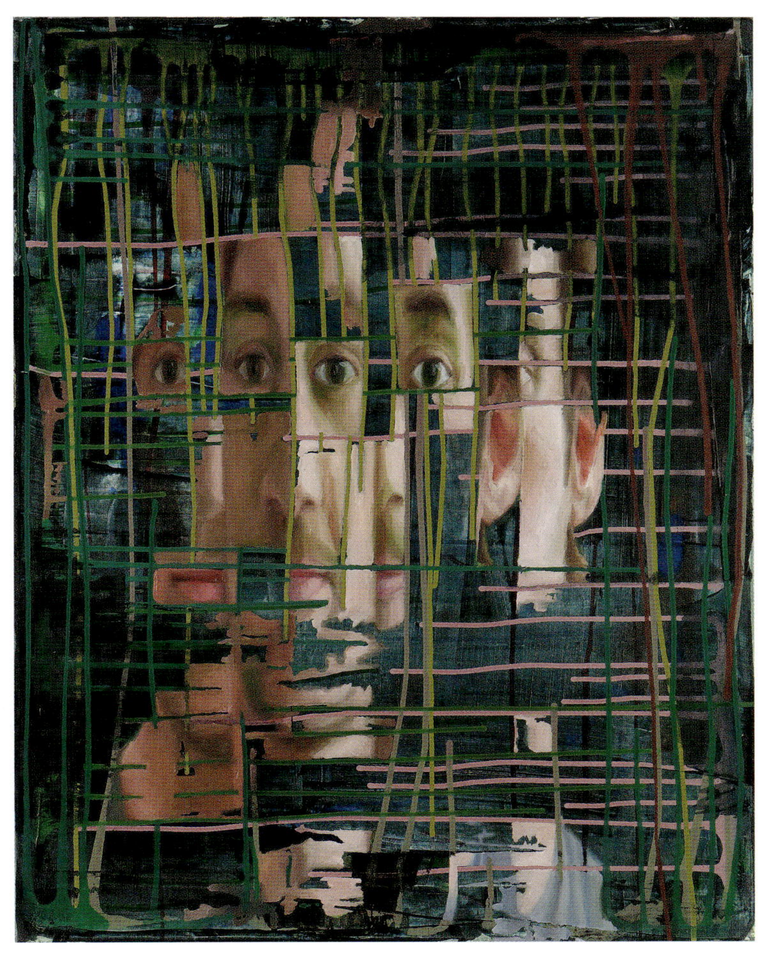

Self-Portrait 2008, 90 x 70 cm, oil and acrylic on canvas, private collection, Budapest

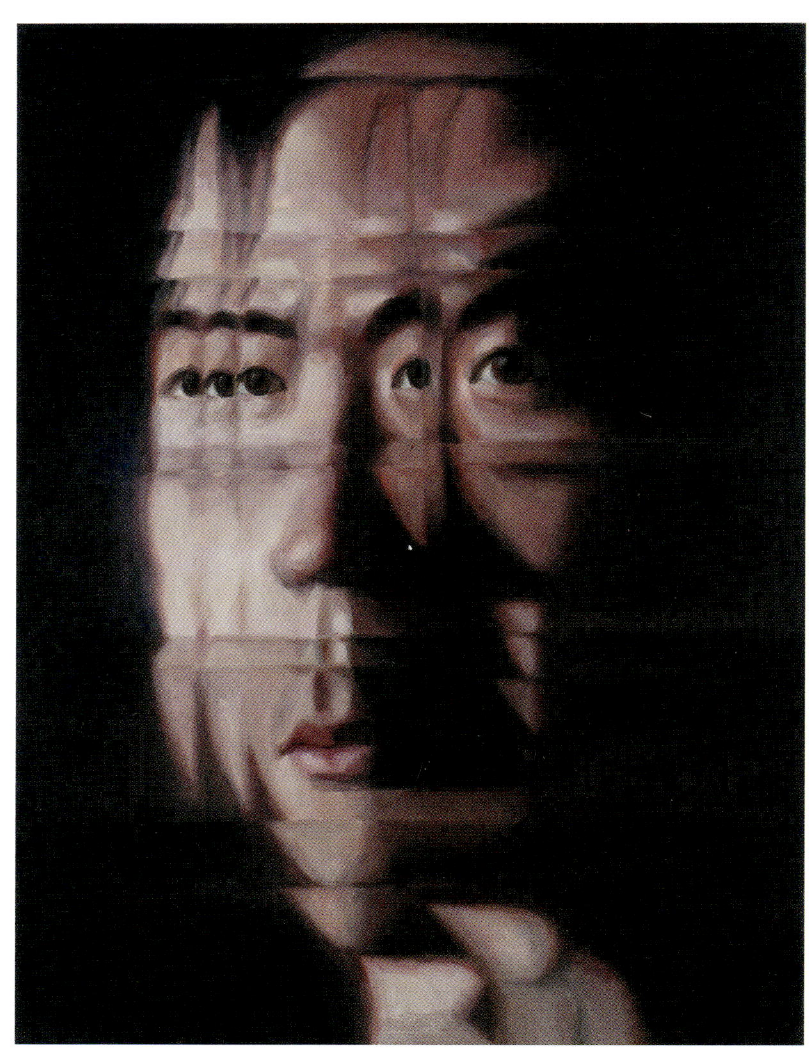

Xiao Xiao 3 2012, 80 x 60 cm, oil on canvas

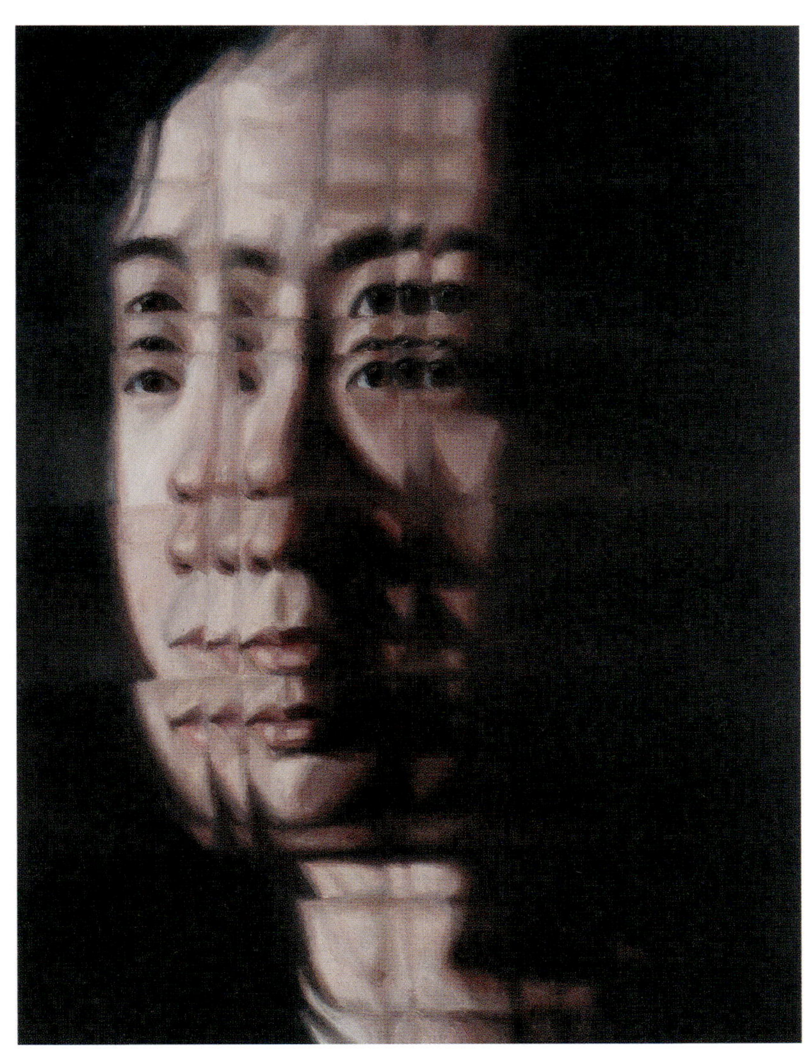

Xiao Xiao 4 2012, 80 x 60 cm, oil on canvas

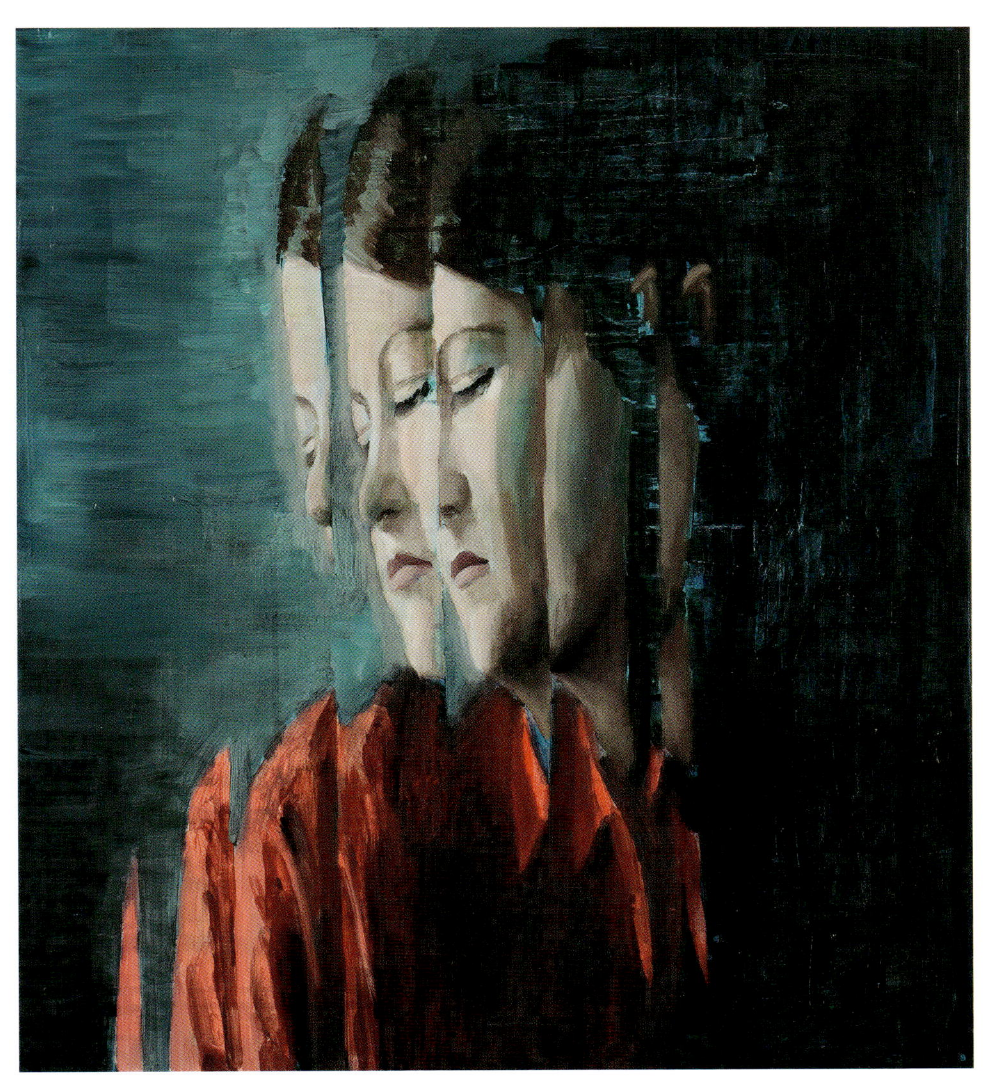

Gwen 2010, 80 x 70 cm, acrylic on canvas, private collection, Berlin

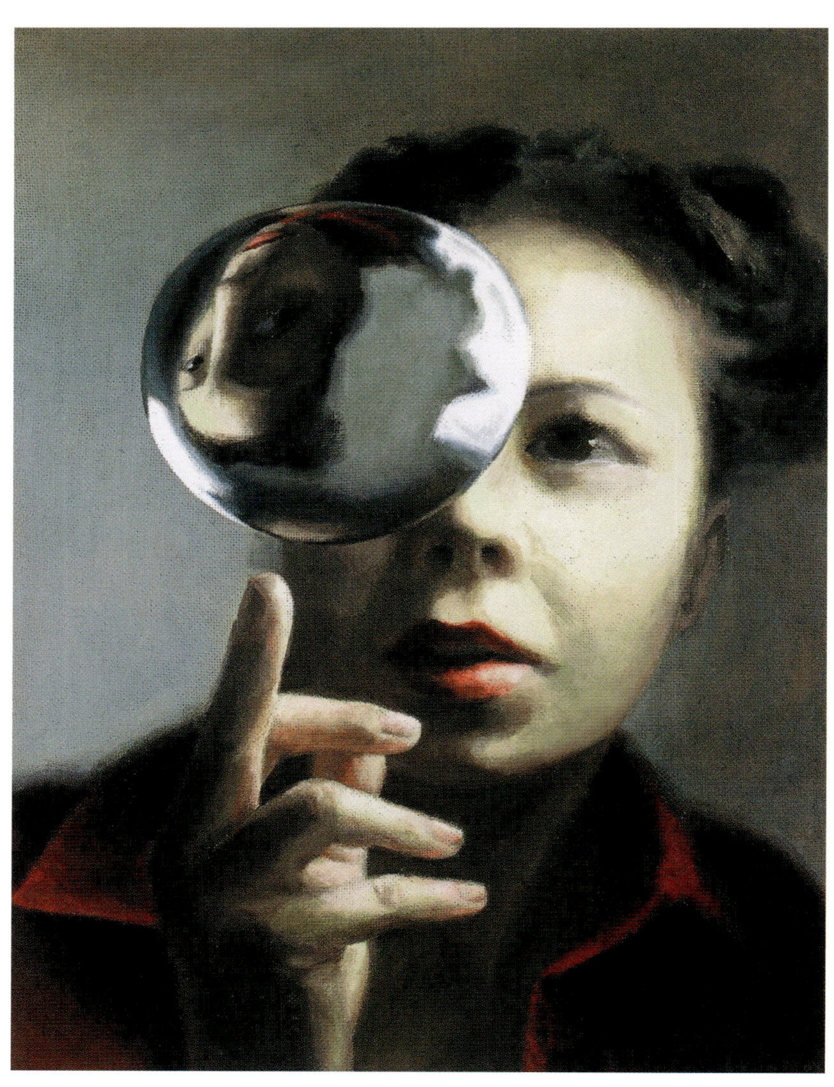

Good Idea 2003, 80 x 60 cm, acrylic on canvas, private collection, Budapest

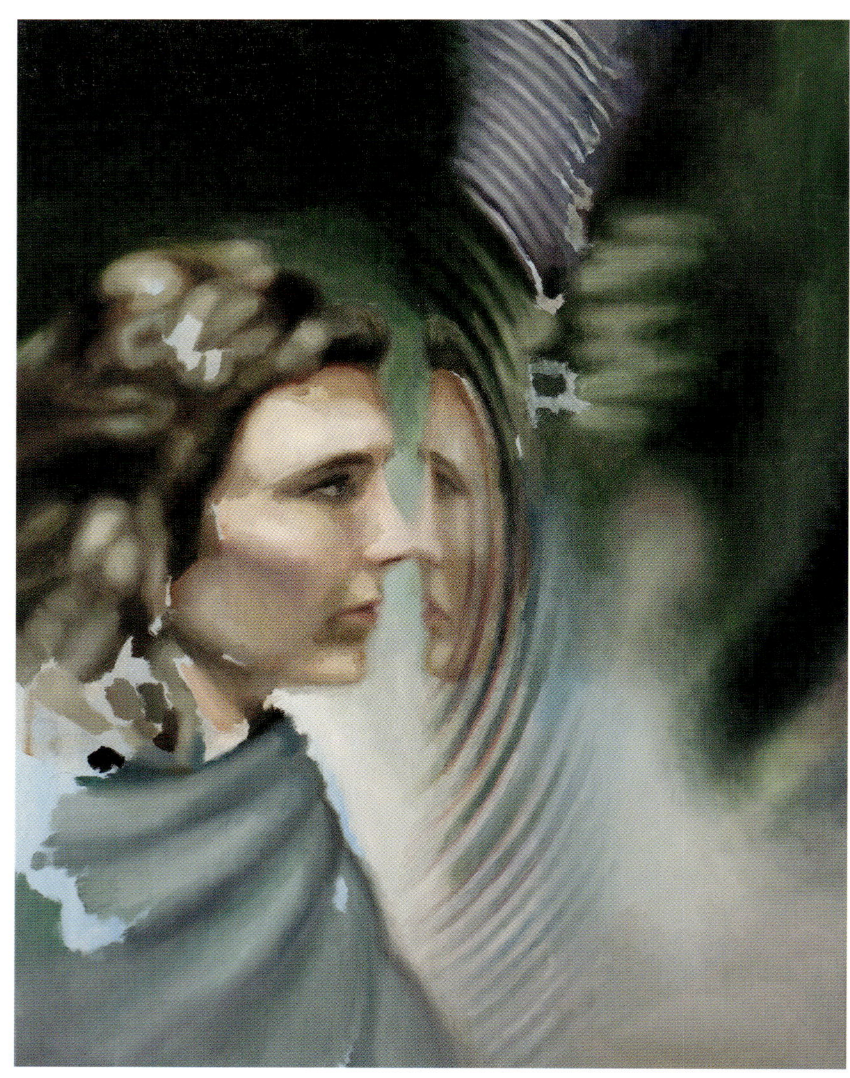

Your Intention 2014, 80 x 60 cm, oil on canvas, Shandong Museum, Jinan, China

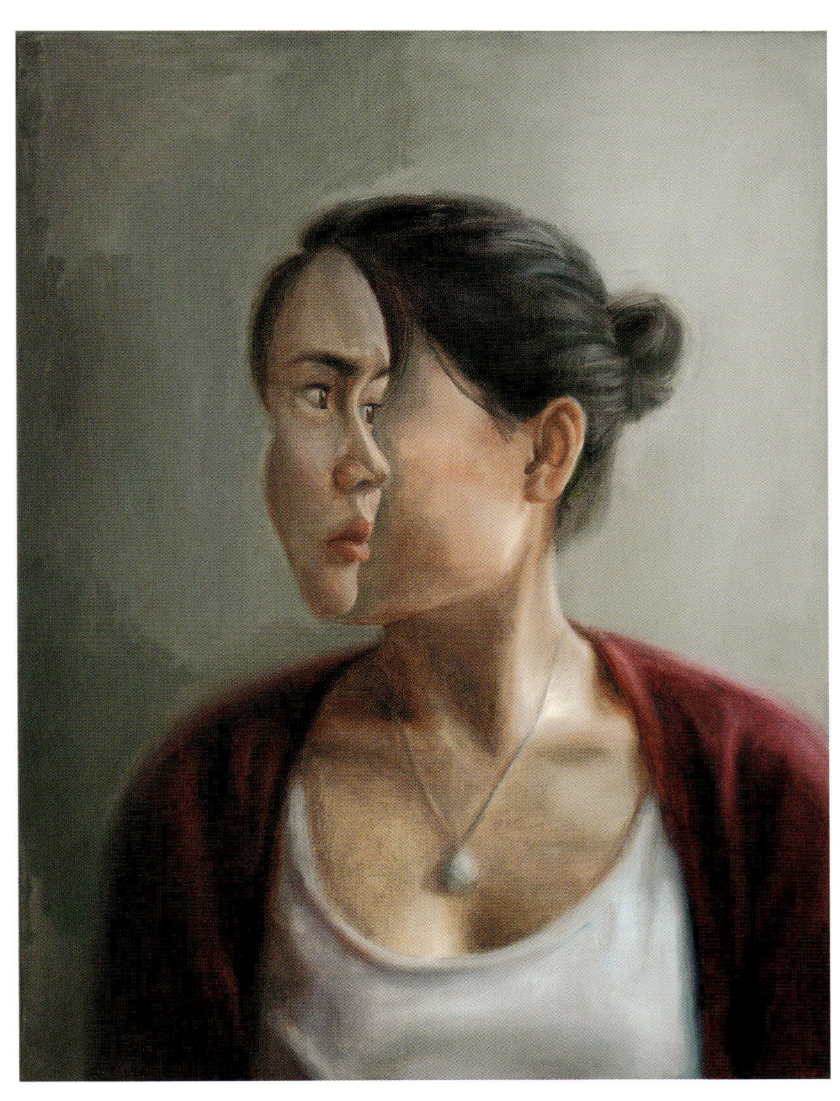

Insight 2014, 80 x 60 cm, oil on canvas

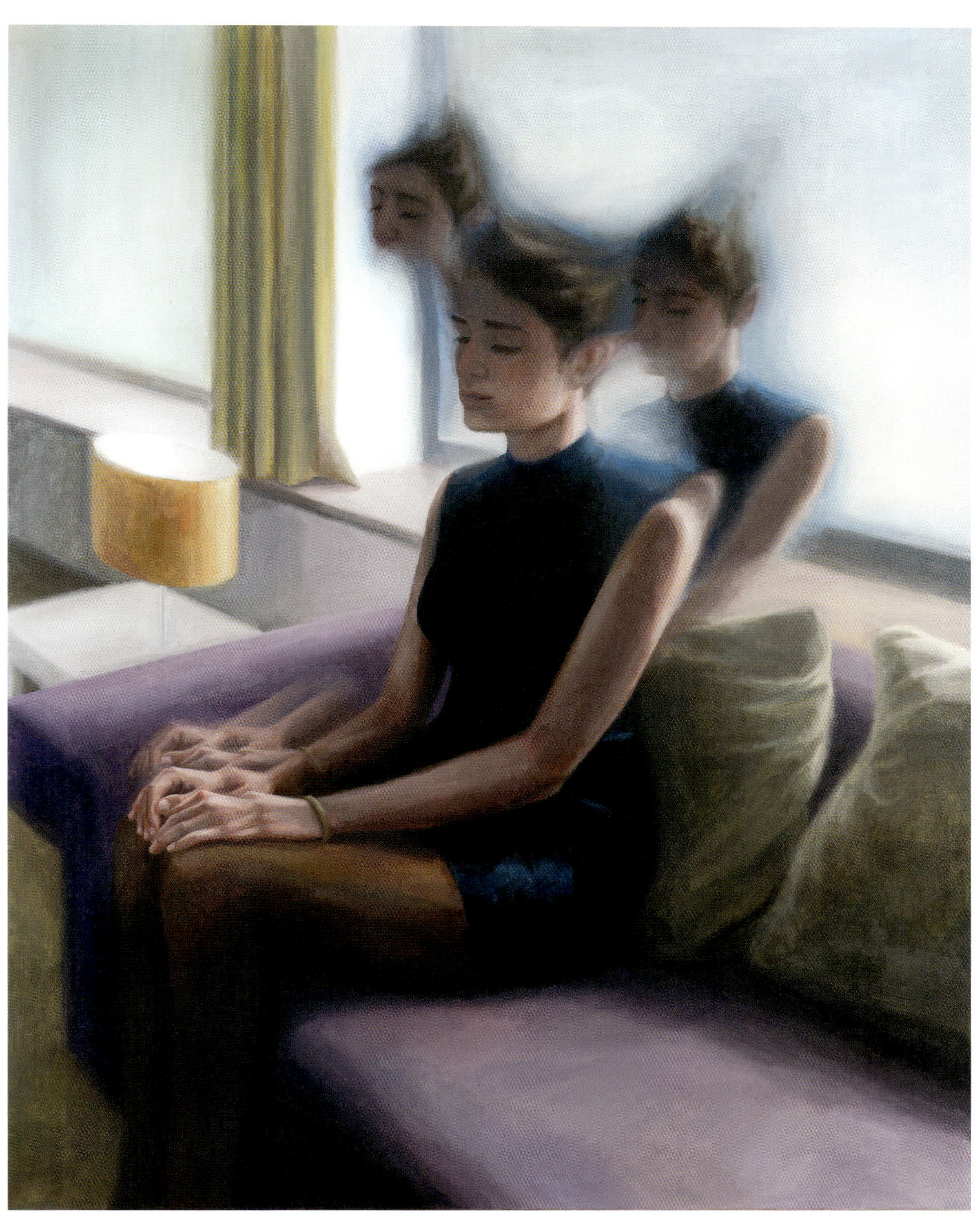

I Am, I Am, I Am 2012, 165 x 130 cm, oil on canvas

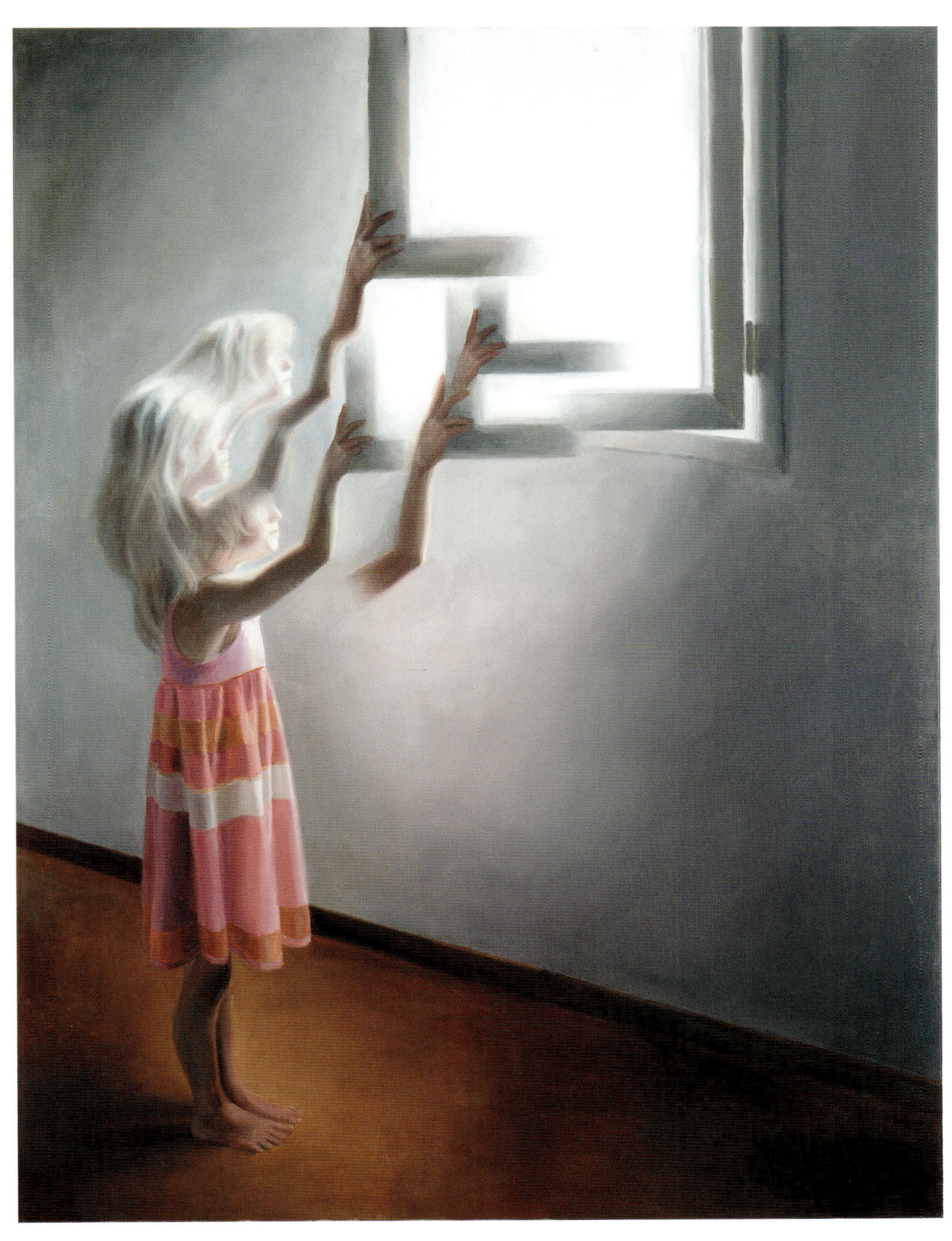

My Life Before Me 2012, 180 x 135 cm, oil on canvas

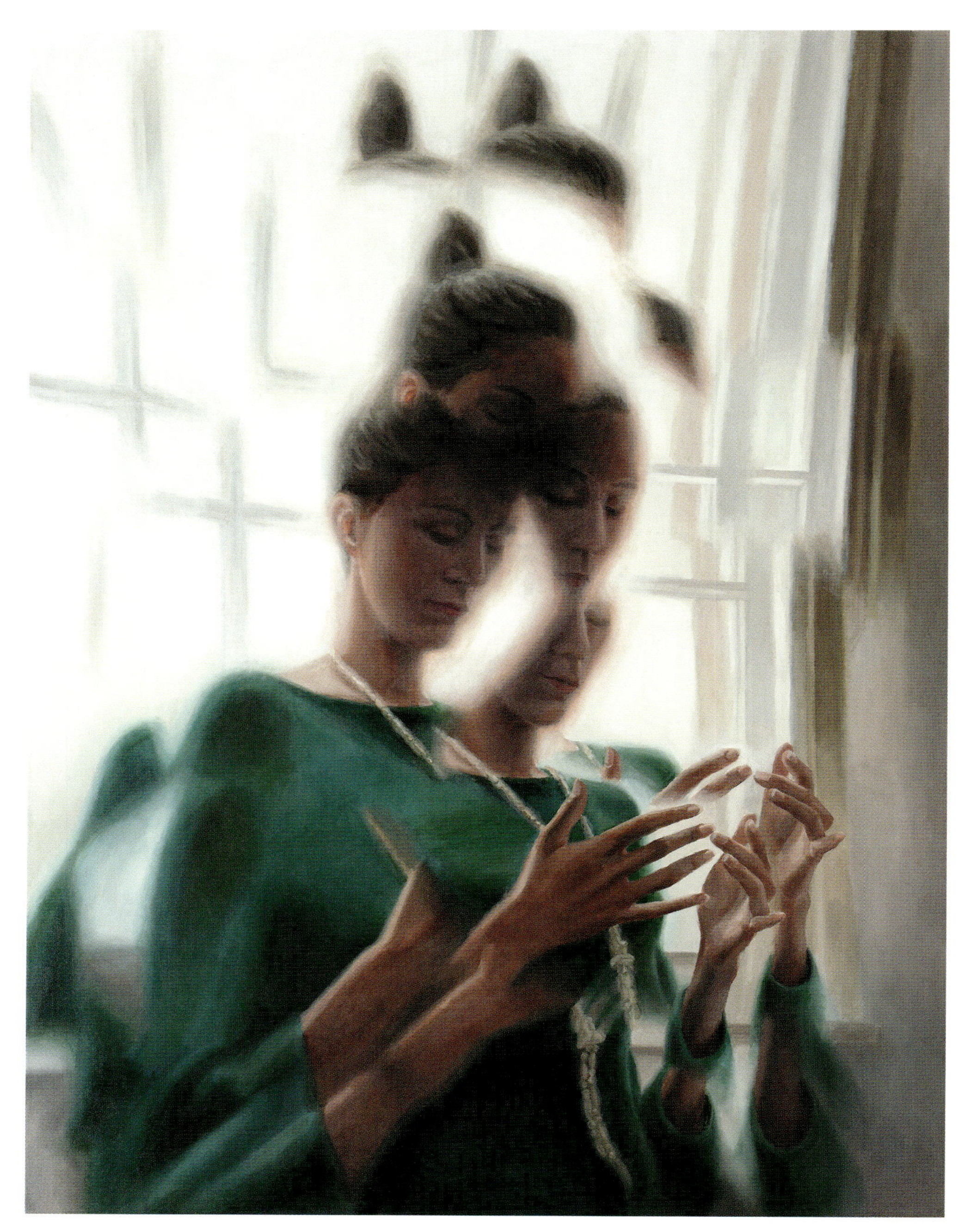

Mind-Body (Gwen) 2012, 140 x 105, oil on canvas

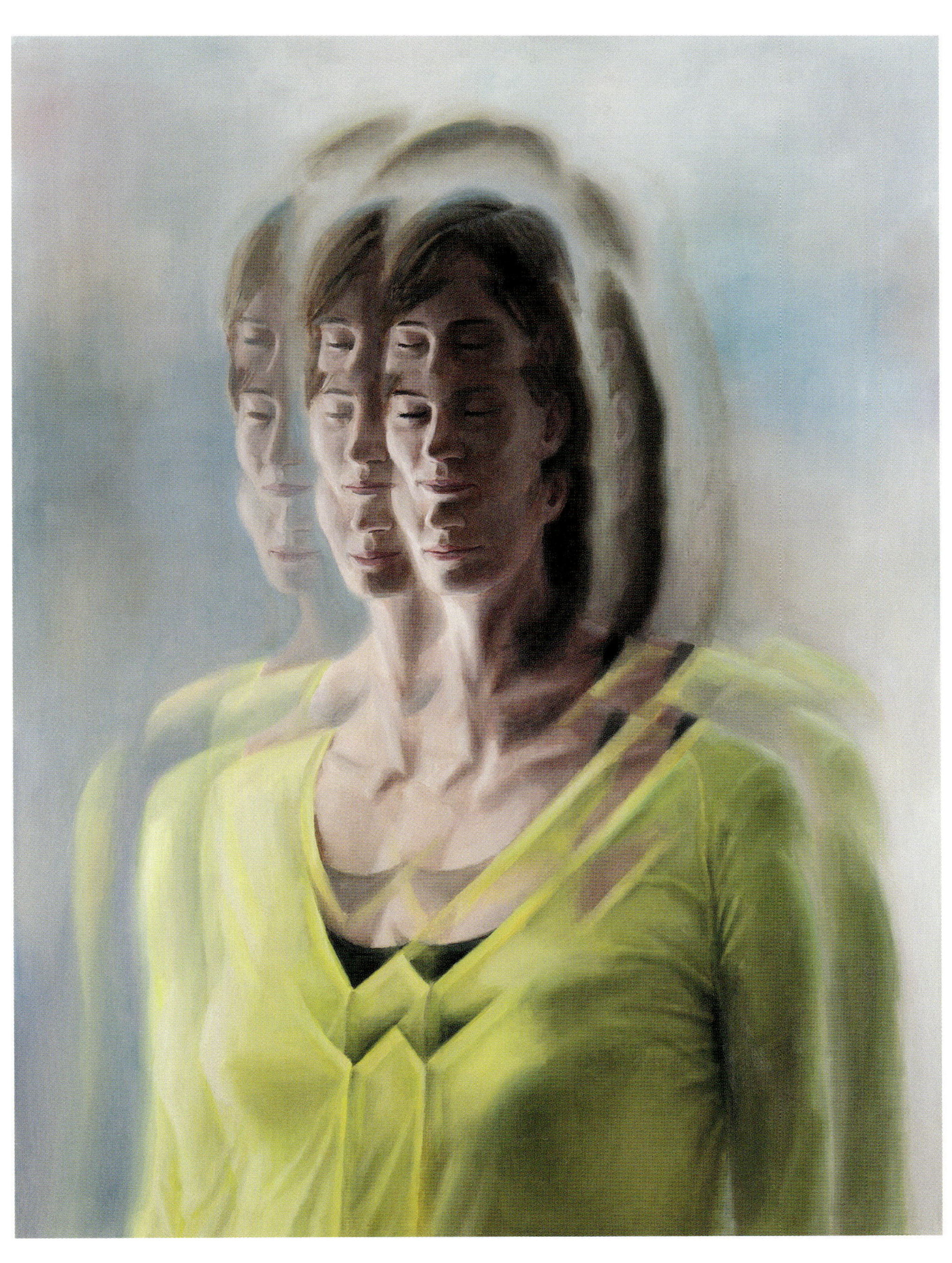

Blink (Jeannine) 2011, 140 x 105, oil on canvas, Biksady Galéria, Budapest

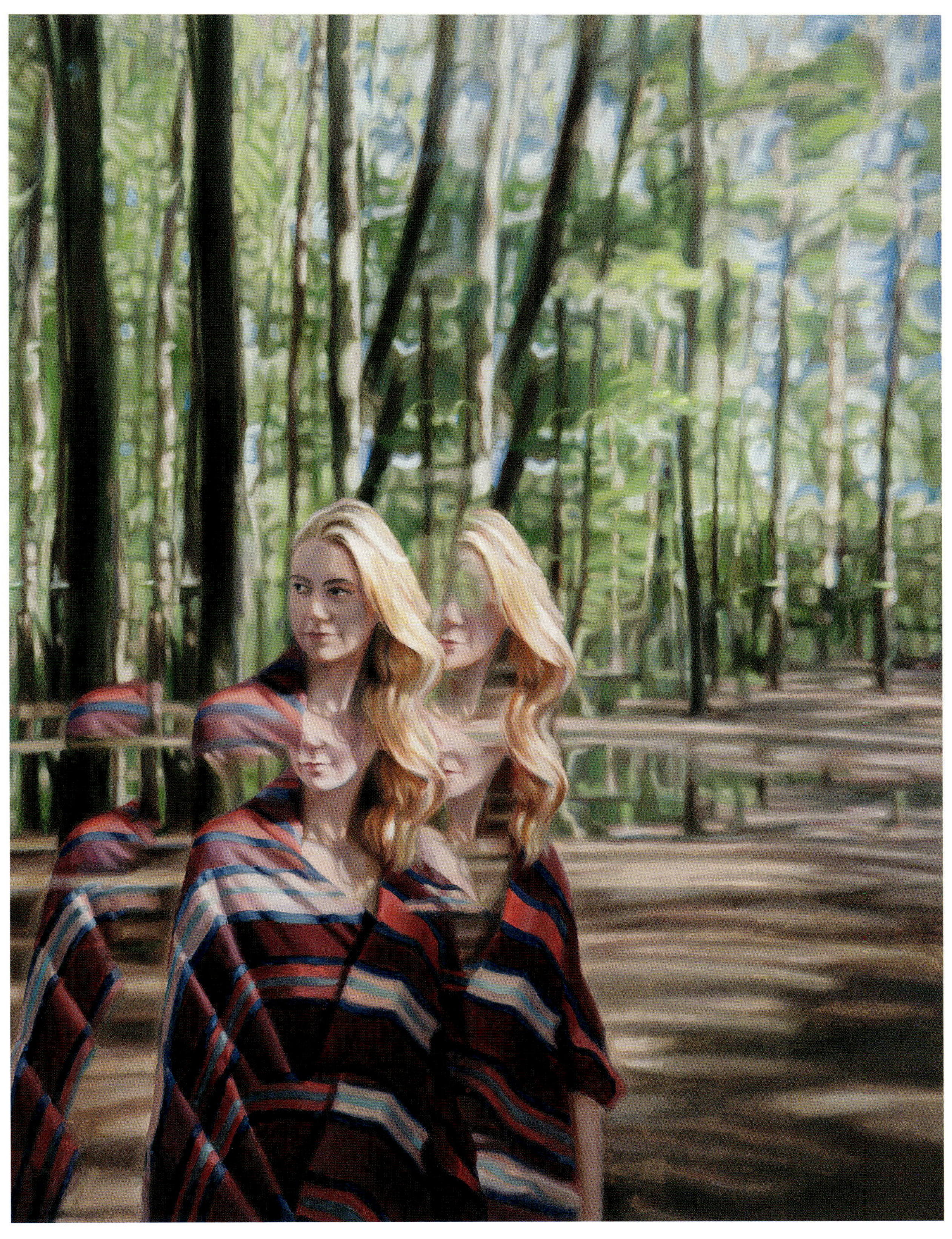

Trip 2012, 200 x 150 cm, oil on canvas

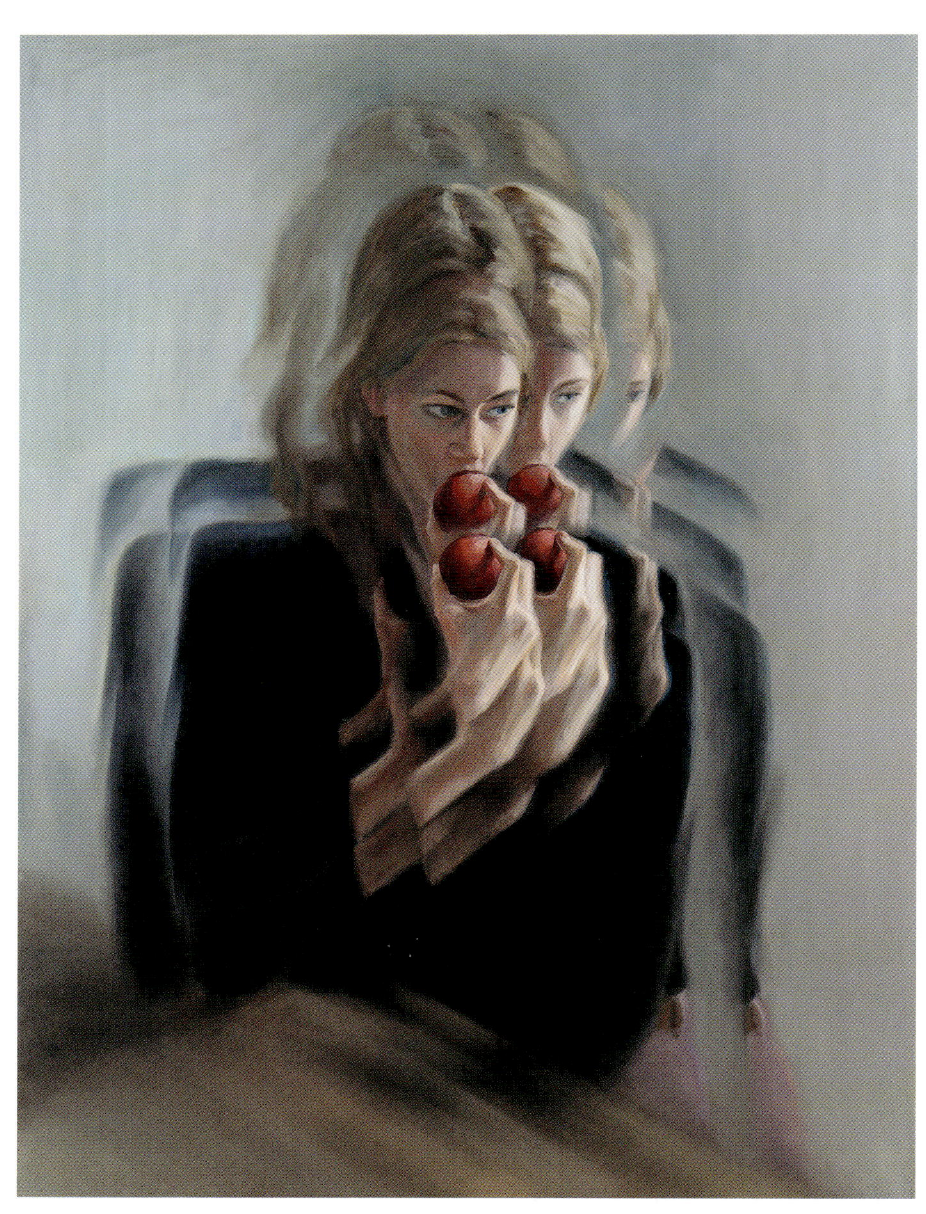

Apple Eater 2012, 140 x 105 cm, oil on canvas, private collection, Istanbul

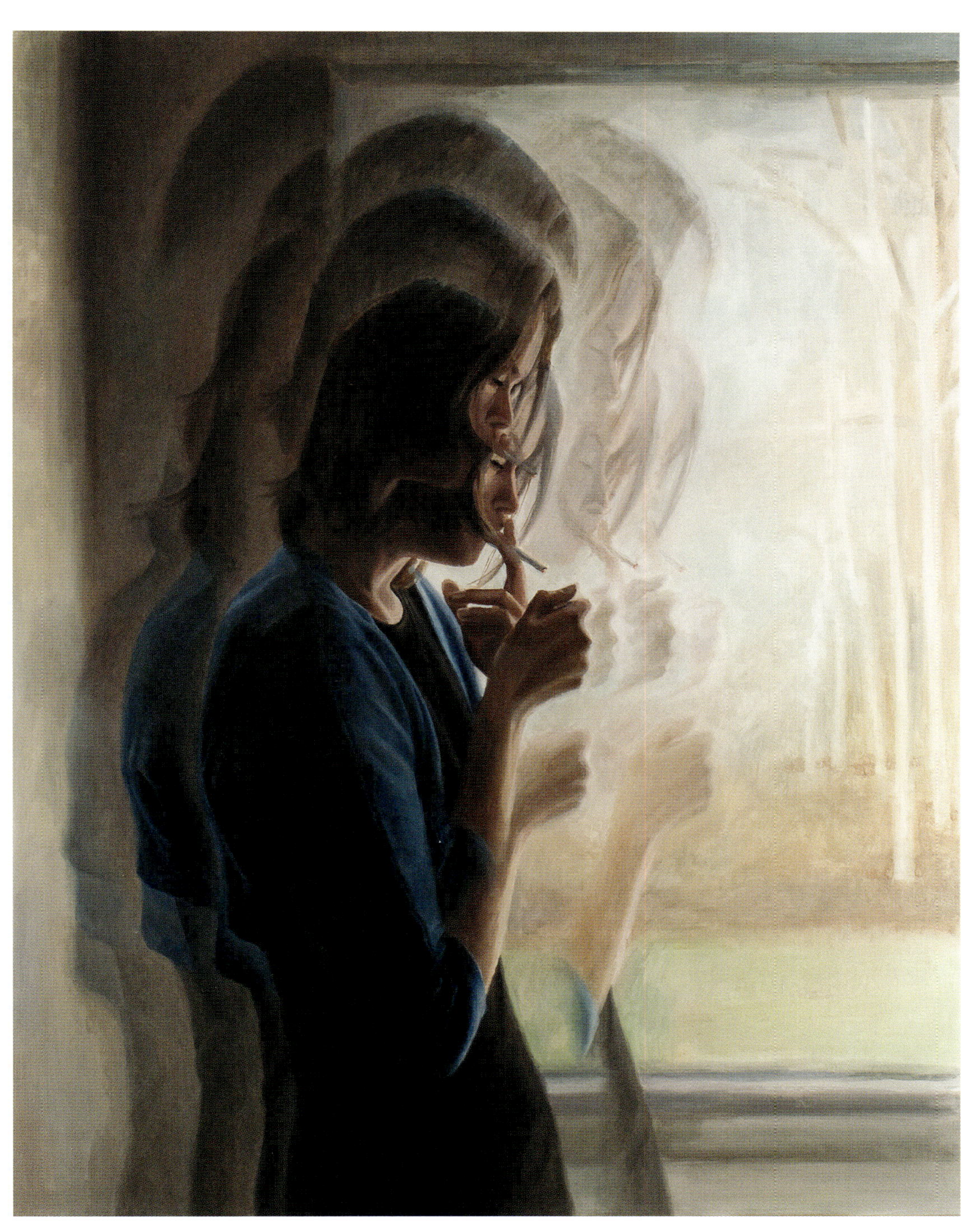

Light Your Fire 2012, 165 x 130 cm, oil on canvas

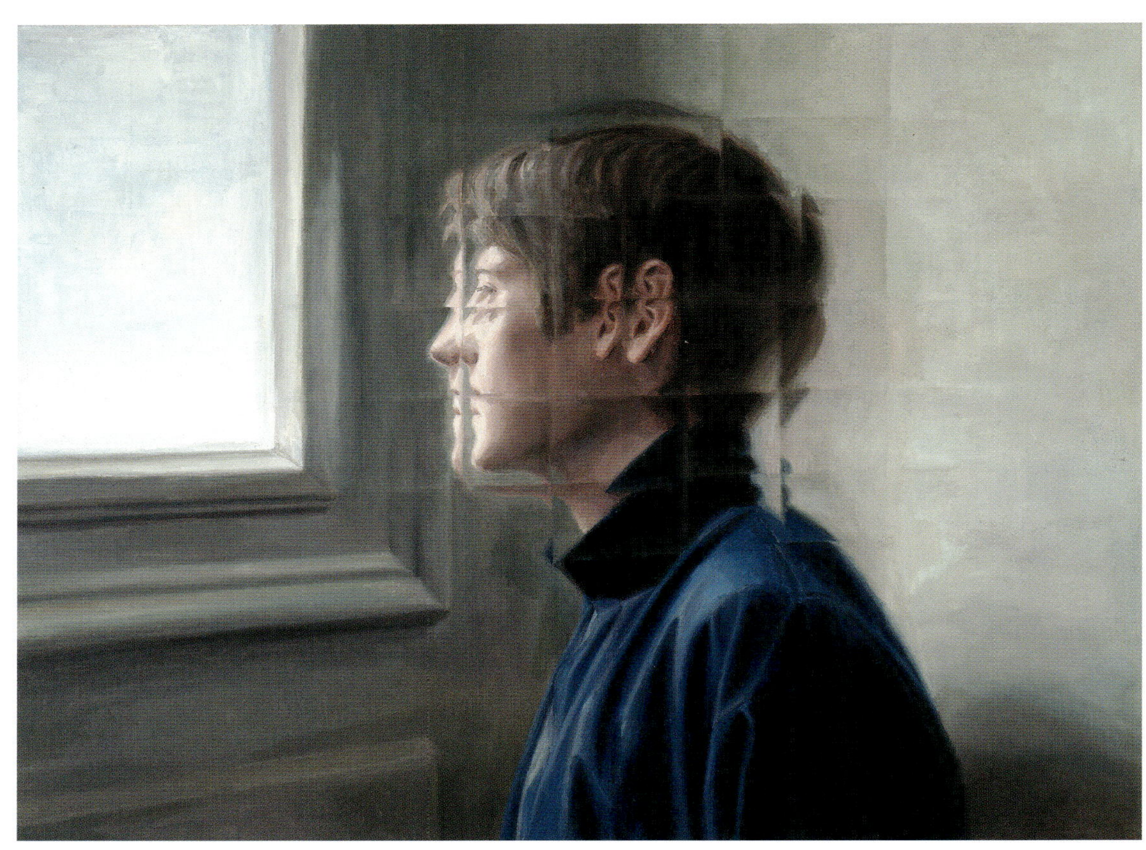

Prospect 2012, 105 x 140 cm, oil on canvas

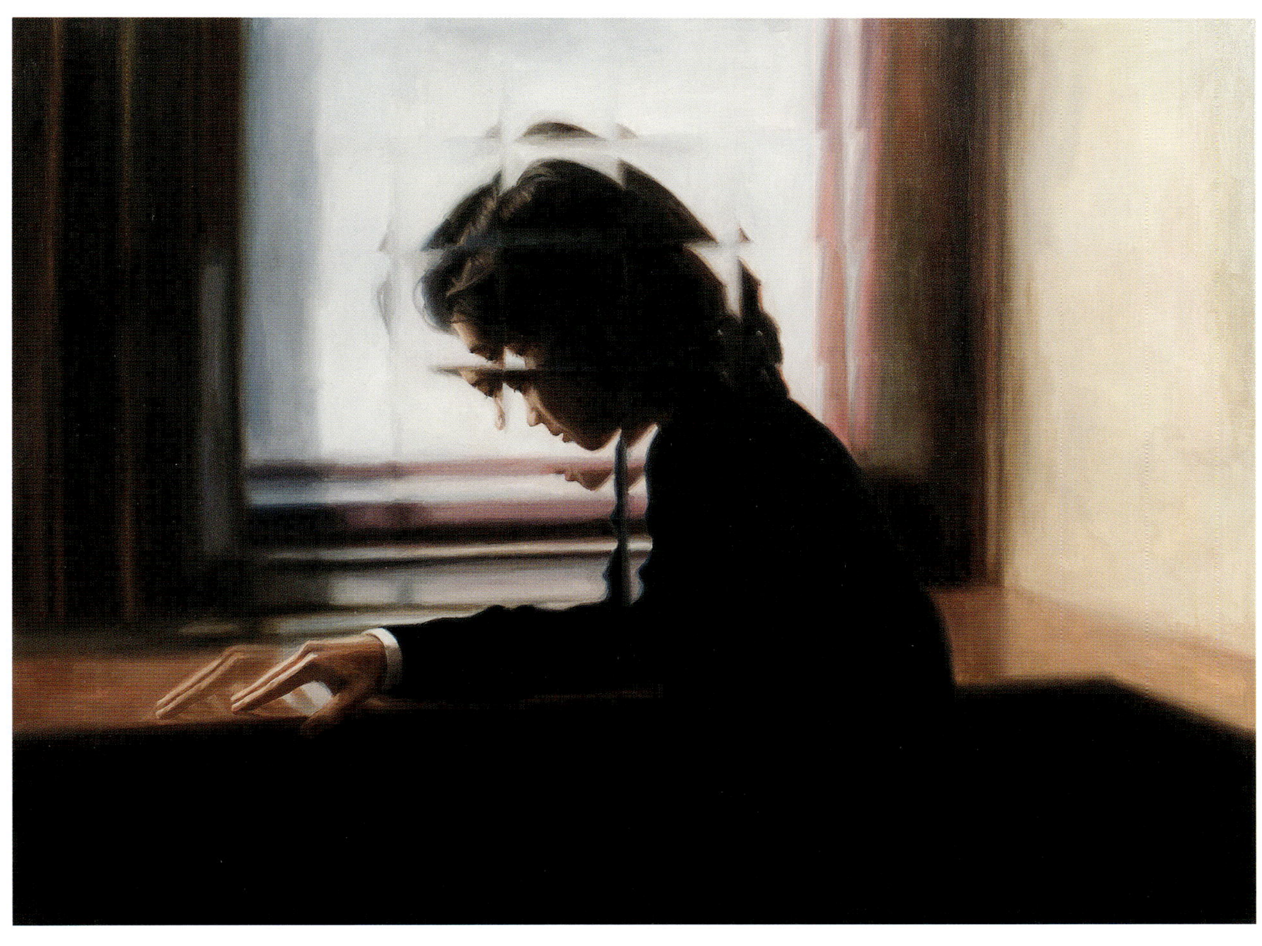

Young Talent 2012, 125 x 165 cm, oil on canvas, private collection, Rotterdam

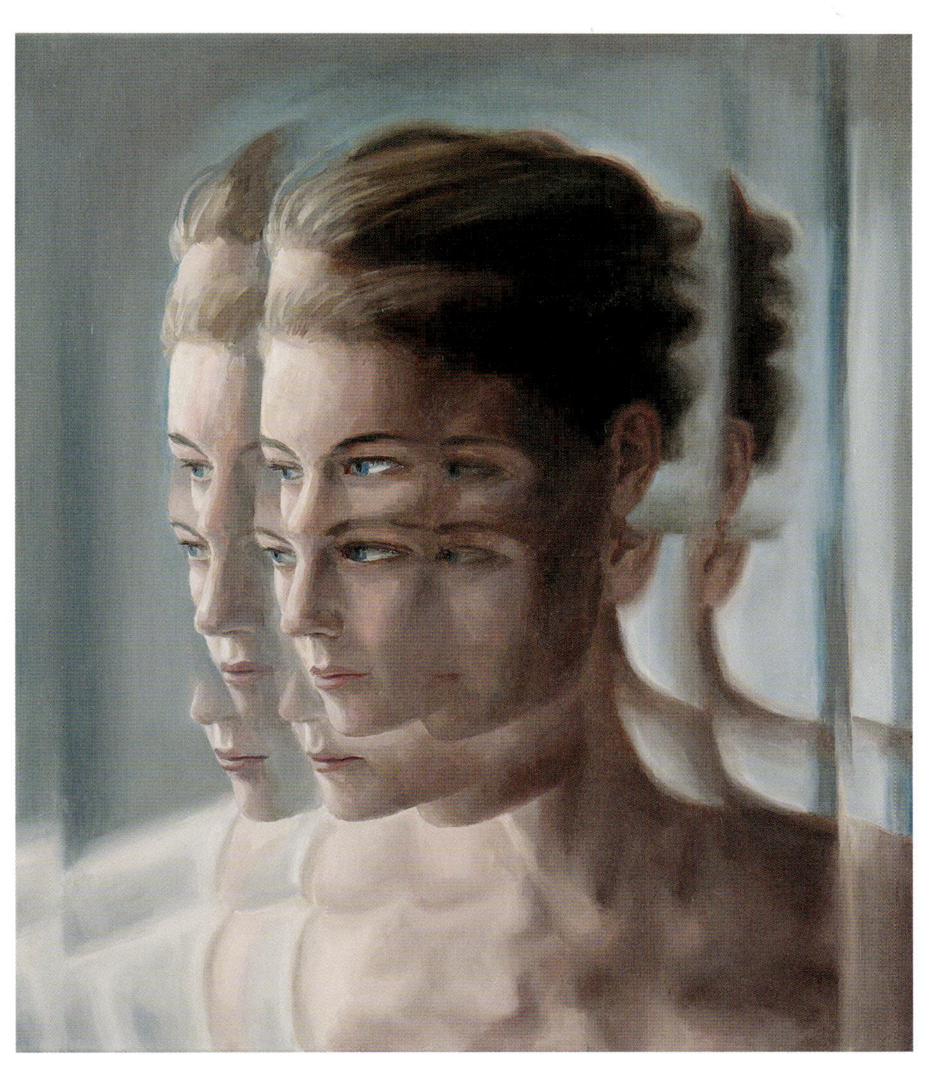

Ksenia 2011, 70 x 60 cm, oil on canvas, private collection, Aalborg

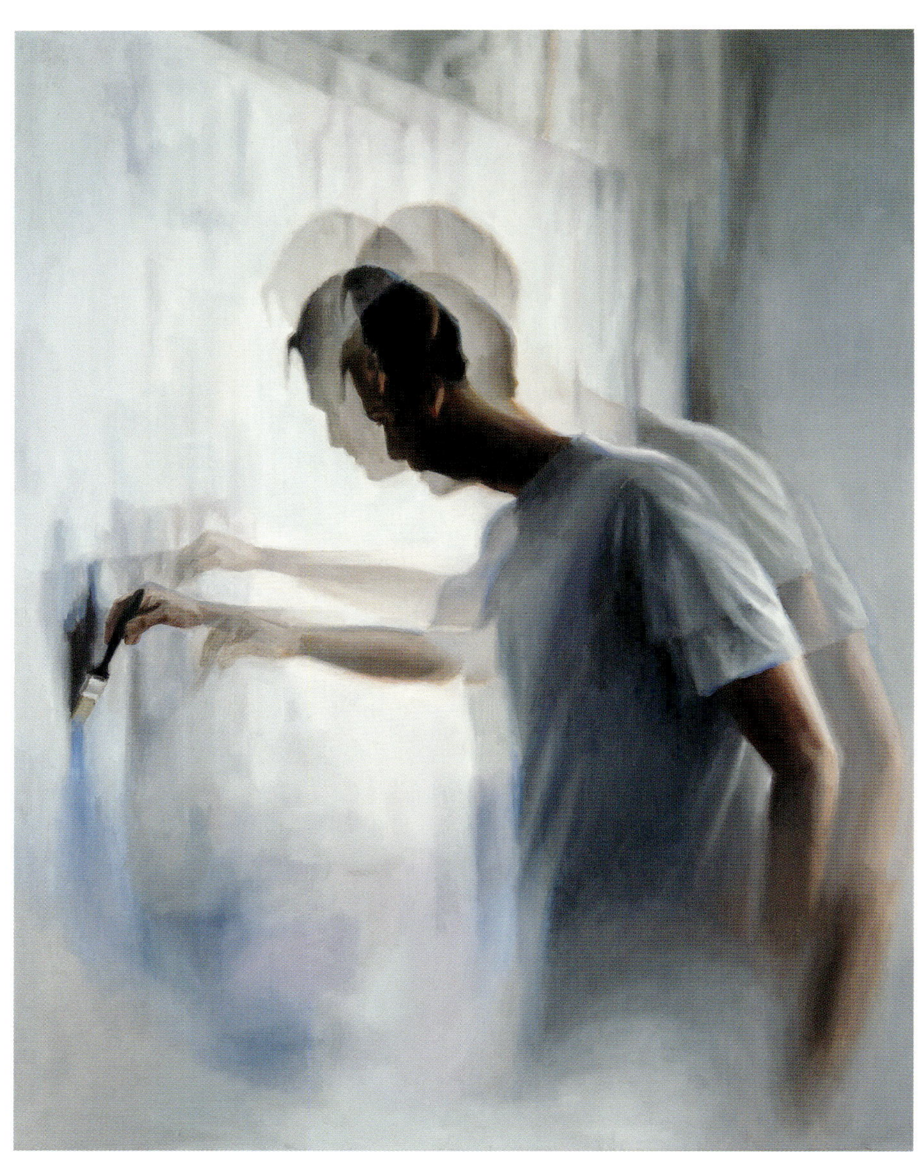

Painter (Max) 2013, 90 x 70 cm, oil on canvas, private collection, Cali, Colombia

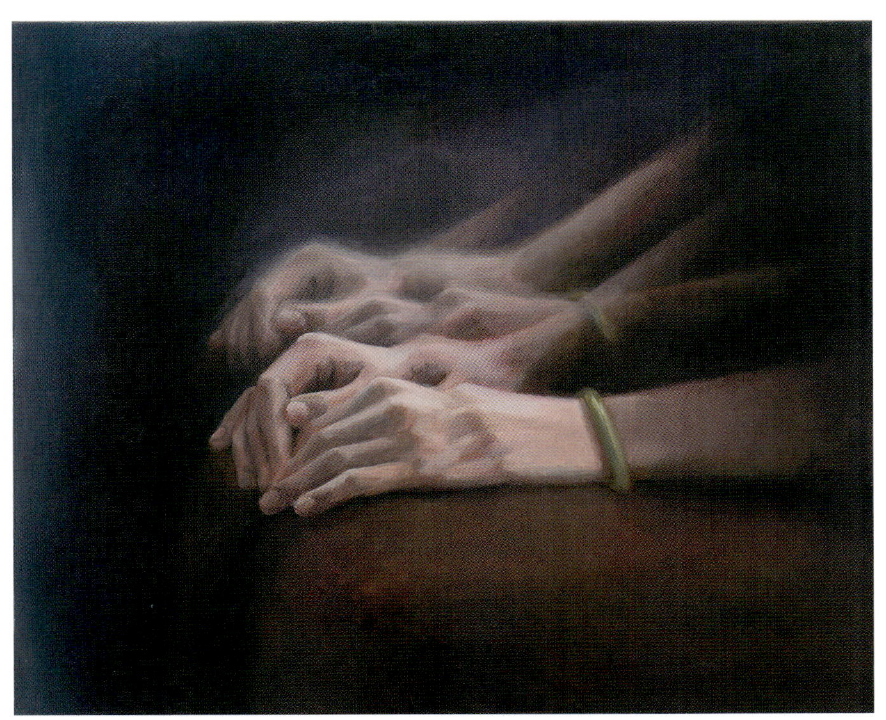

Hands 2012, 50 x 60 cm, oil on canvas, private collection, Berlin

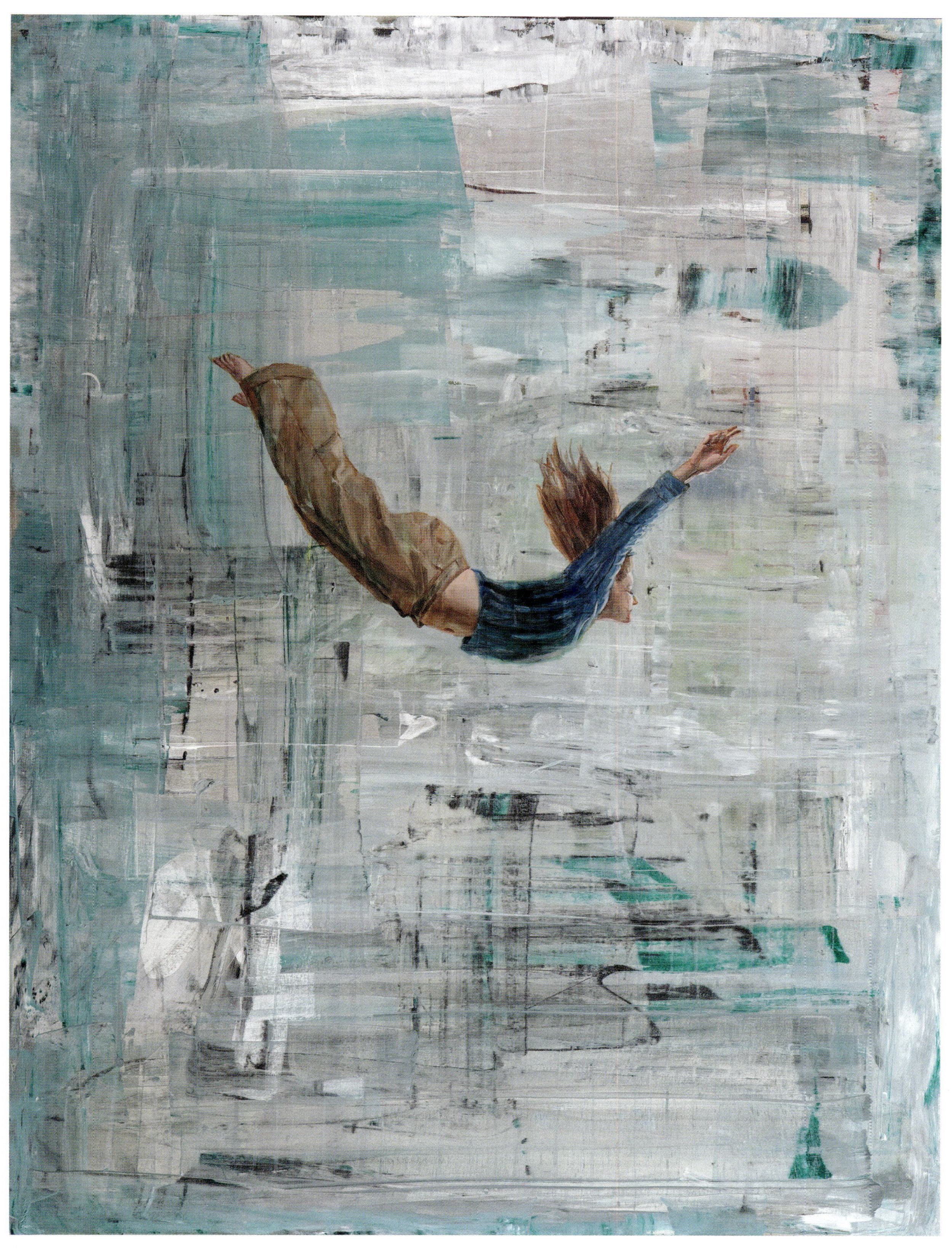

In the Now 2010, 200 x 150 cm, acrylic on canvas, private collection, Düsseldorf

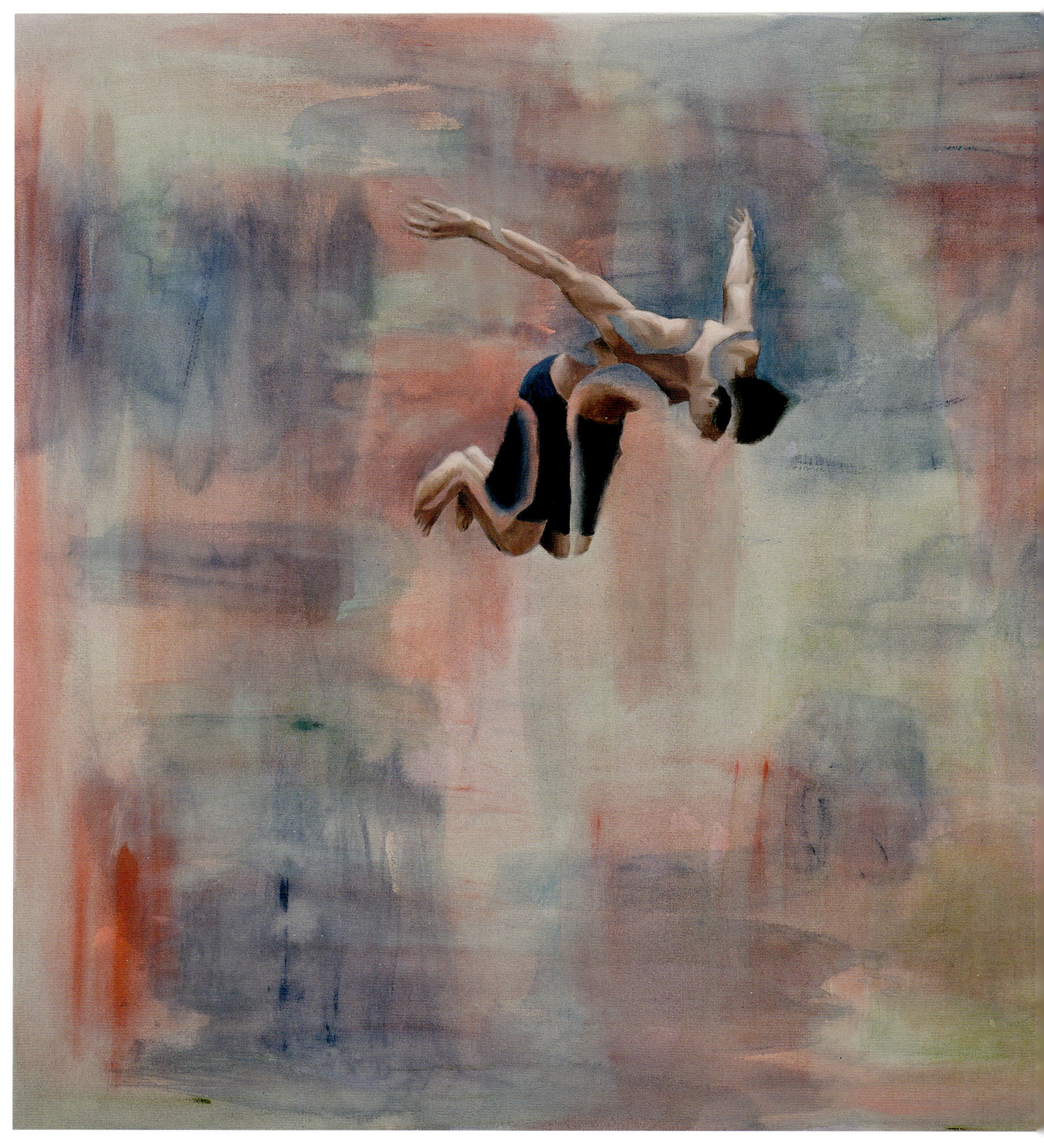

Falling Apart 2016, 130 x 180 cm, acrylic and oil on canvas

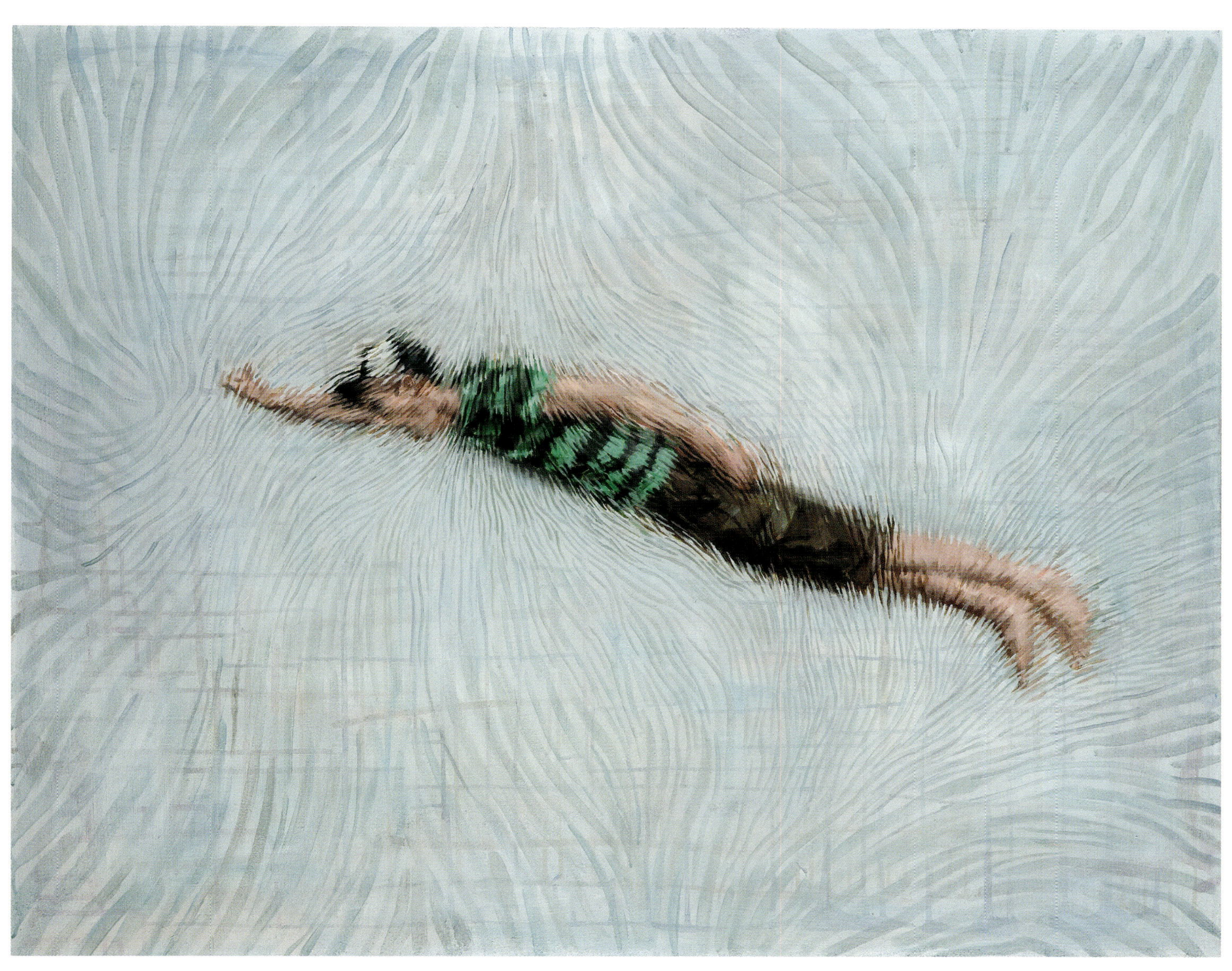

The Power 2009, 102 x 128 cm, acrylic on canvas, private collection, Vienna

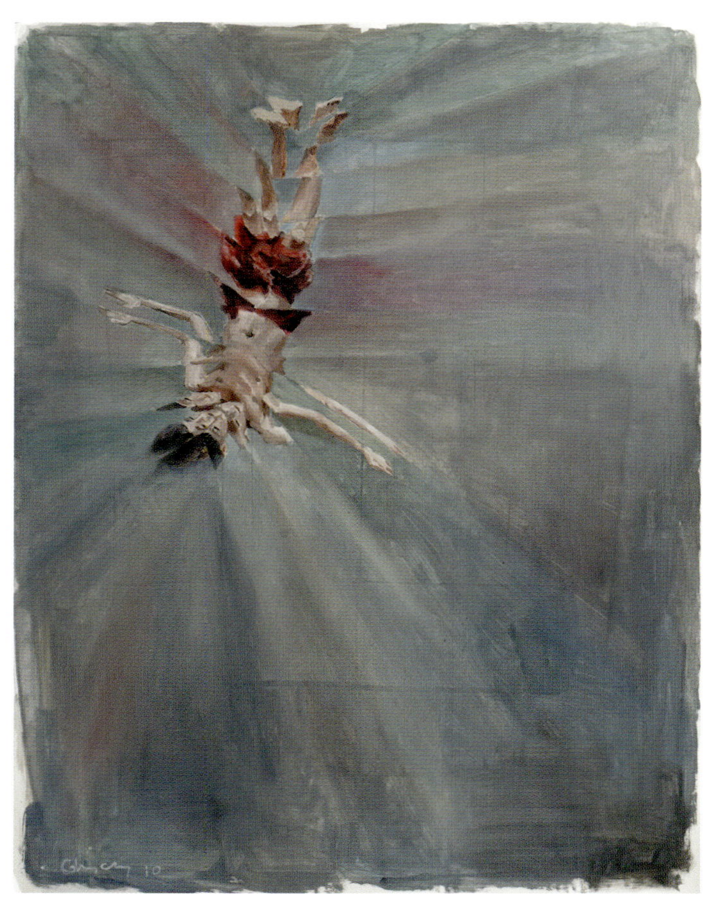

Crash 2010, 65 x 50 cm, oil on paper

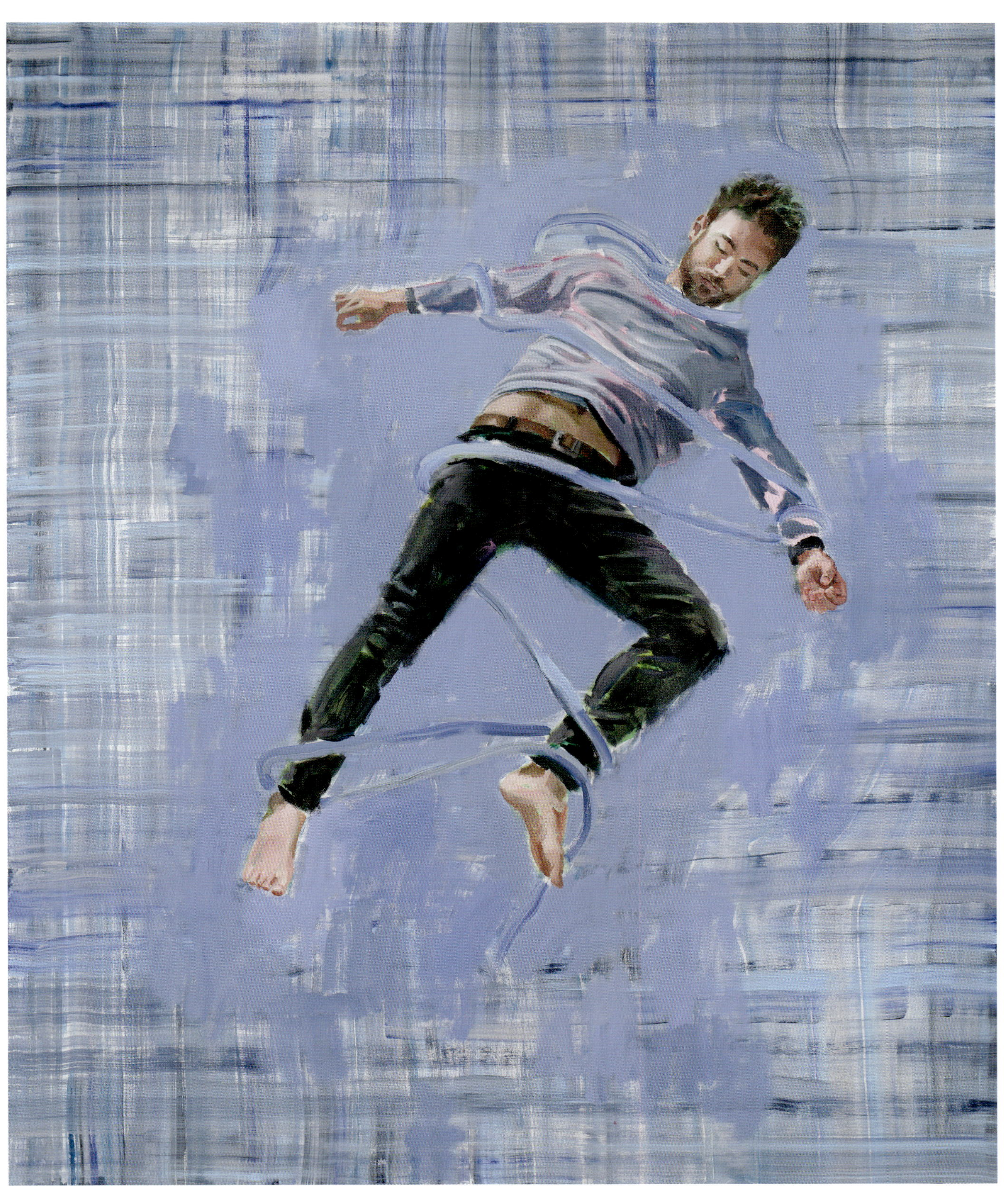

Ground Control 2016, 200 x 150 cm, oil and acrylic on canvas

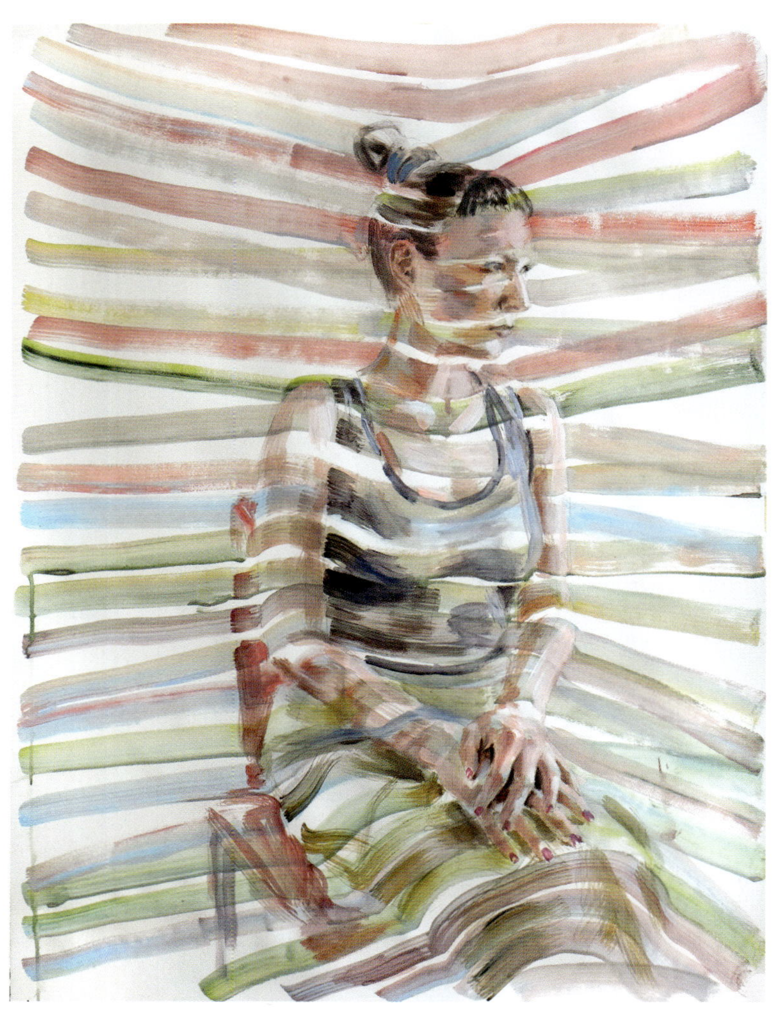

Strapped 2015, 76 x 56 cm, acrylic on paper, private collection, Buenos Aires

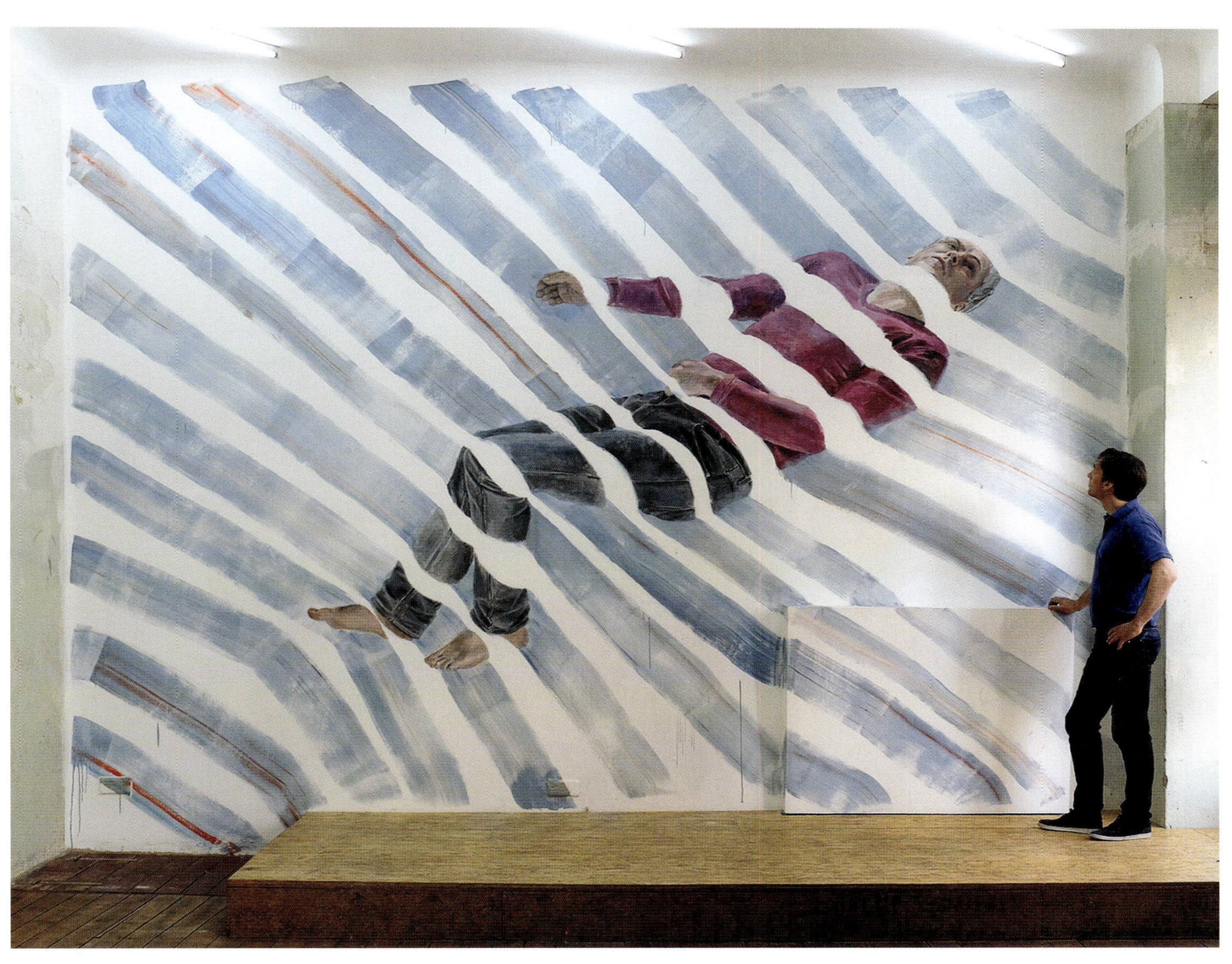

Temporary Mural 2015, 4 x 5 m, acrylic, povvera project space, Berlin

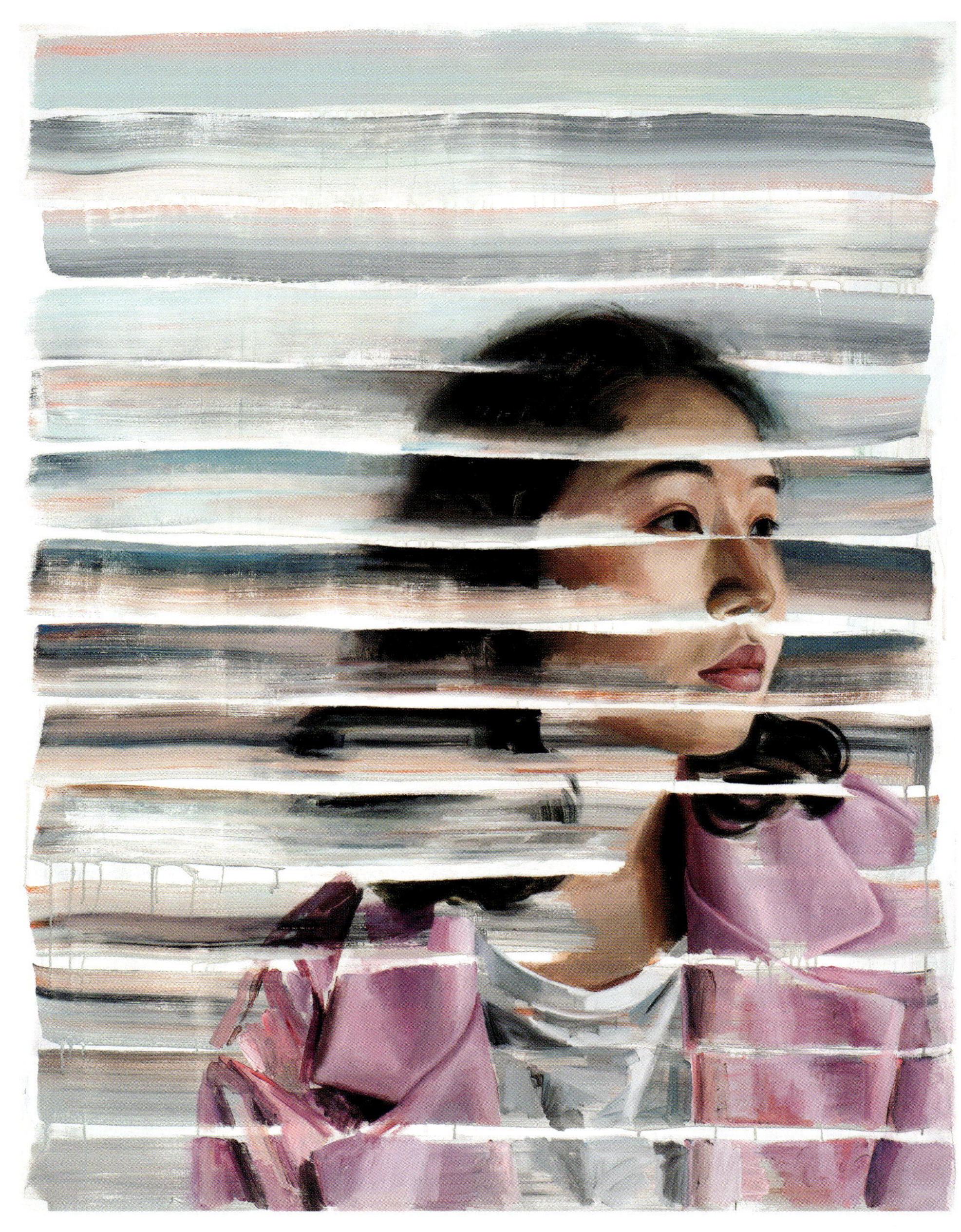

What's Your Frequency? 2014, 165 x 125 cm, acrylic and oil on canvas

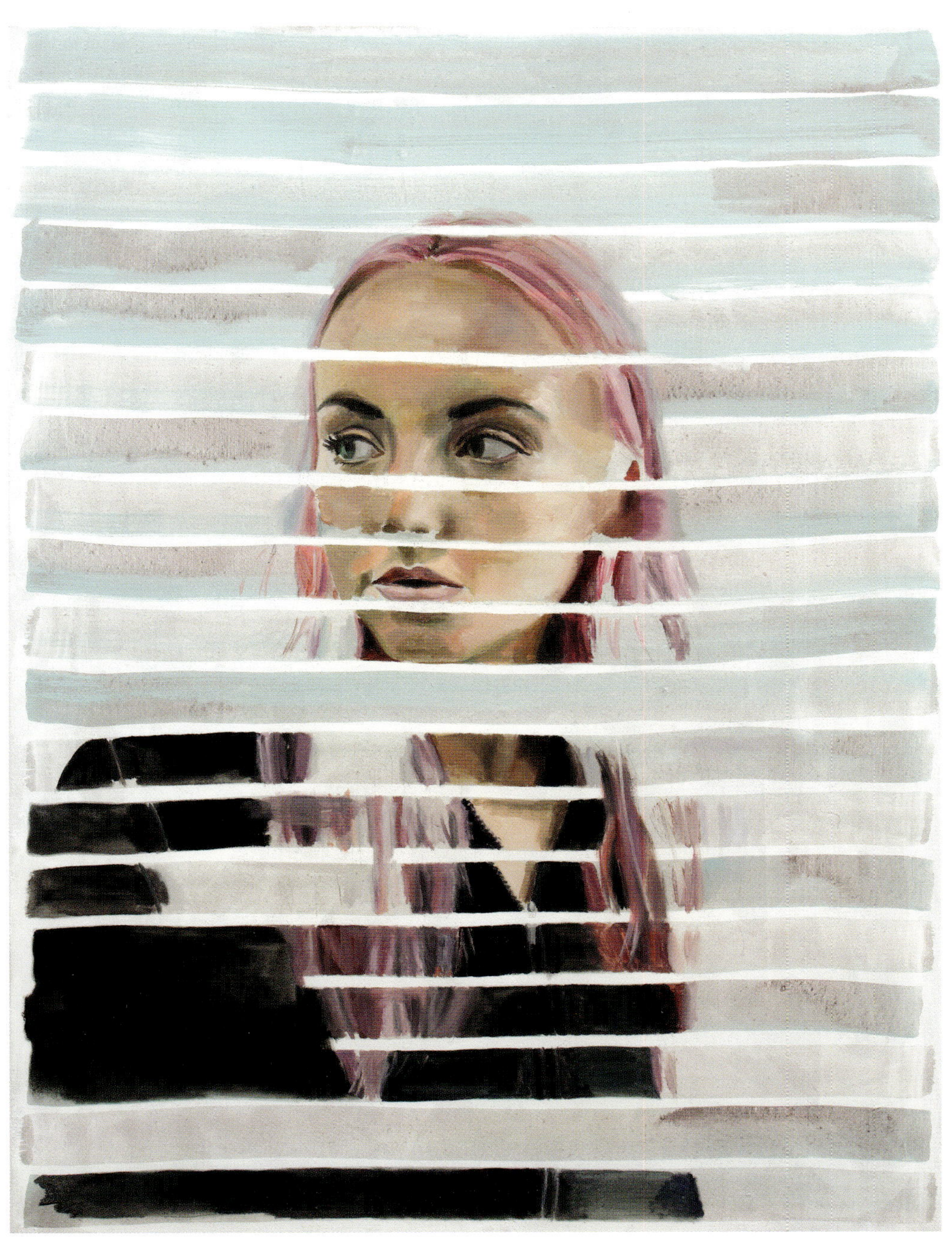

Lily's Hair 2014, 160 x 120 cm, acrylic and oil on canvas

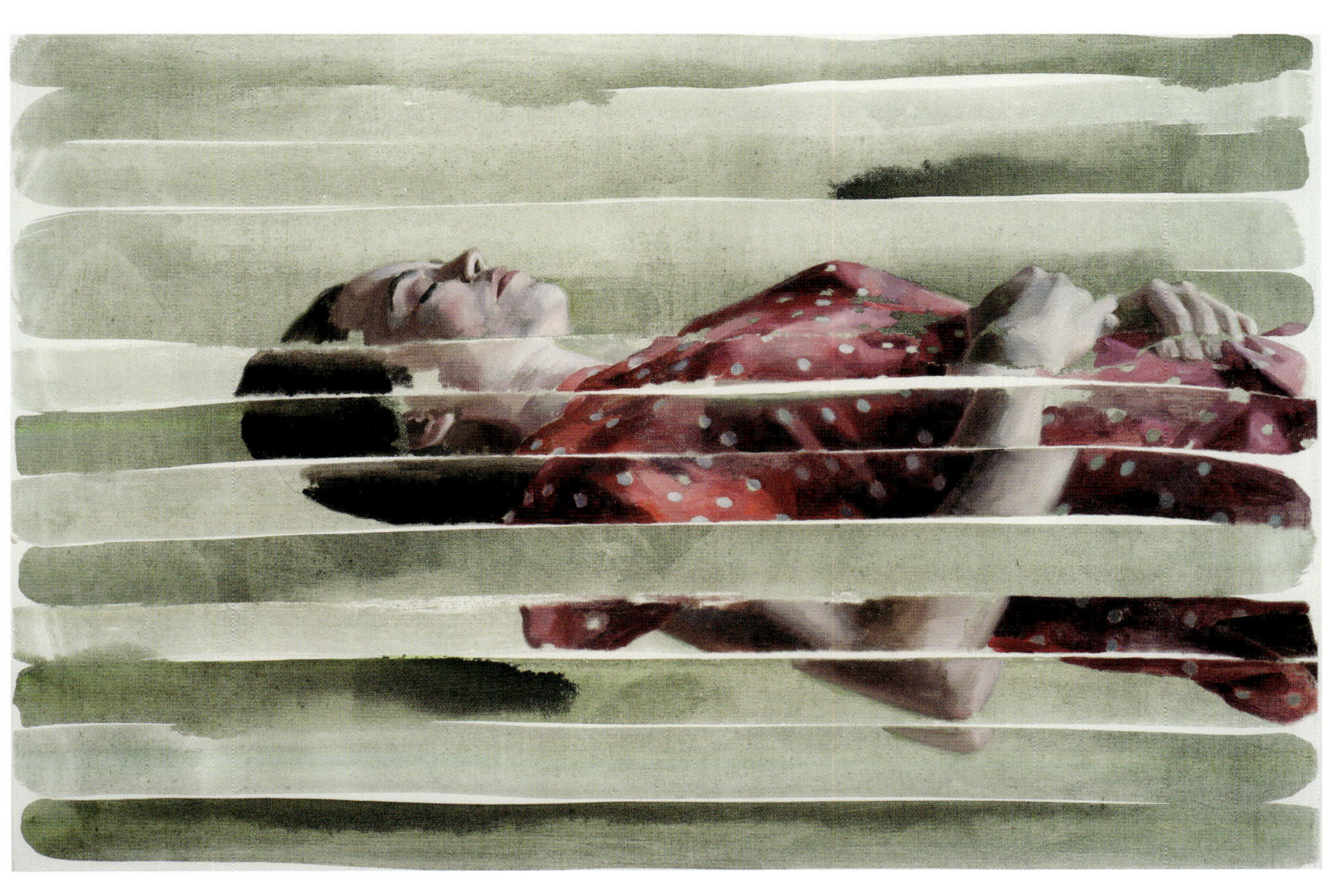

Lucid Dream 2014, 90 x 135 cm, acrylic and oil on canvas

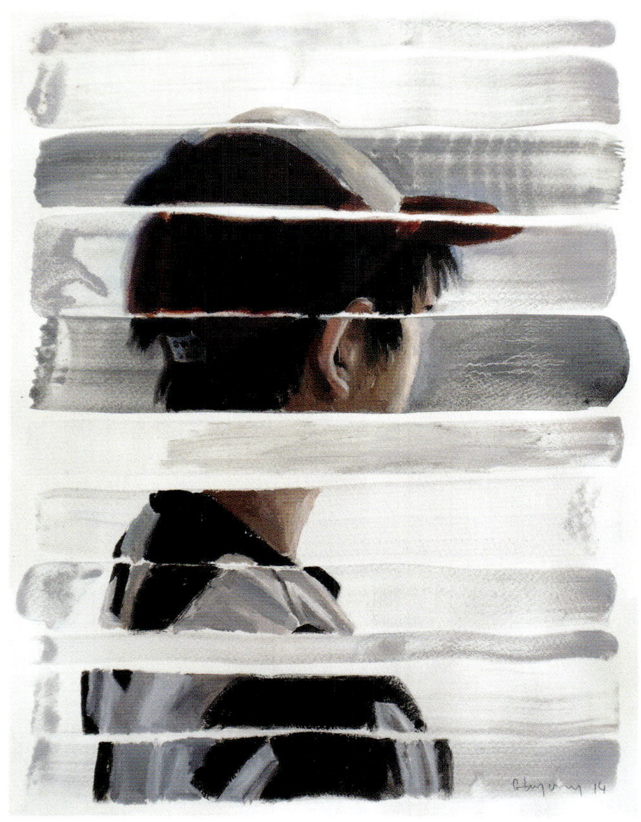

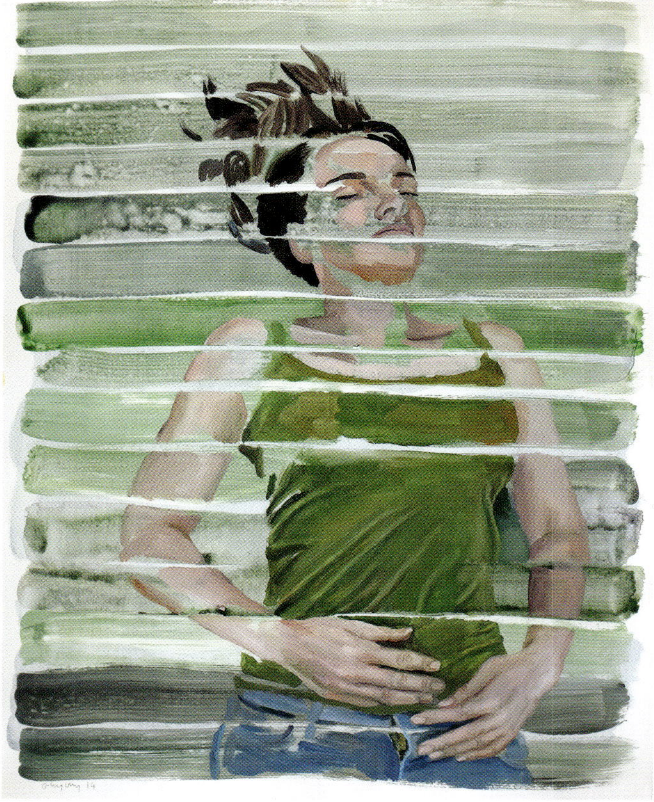

Boy with Cap 2014, 40 x 30 cm, acrylic on paper, private collection, Holland

Deeper Layers 2014, 66 x 50 cm, acrylic on paper, private collection, Buenos Aires

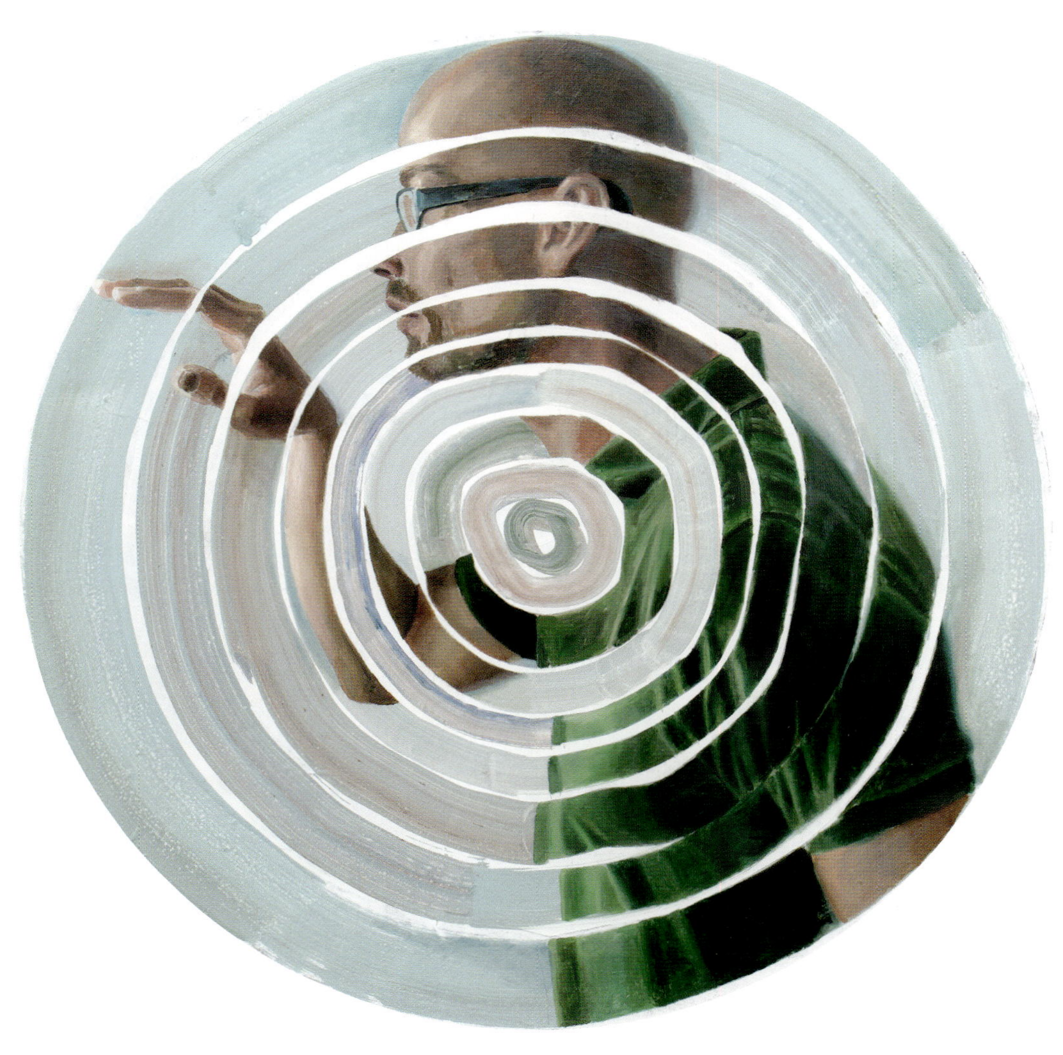

Seeing Is Believing 2014, ∅ 120 cm, oil on canvas

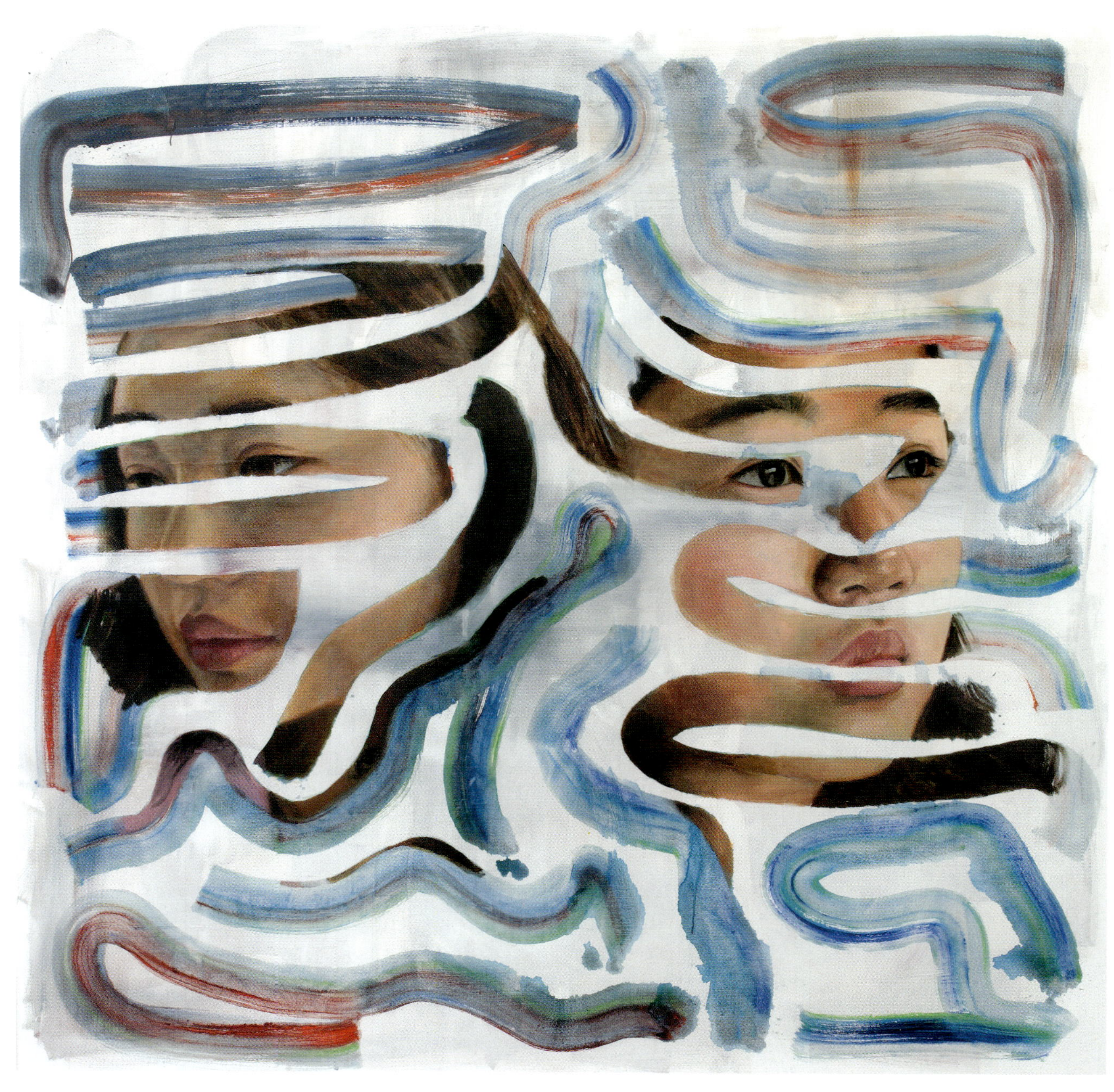

Two Faces of Momo 2014, 200 x 200 cm, acrylic and oil on canvas

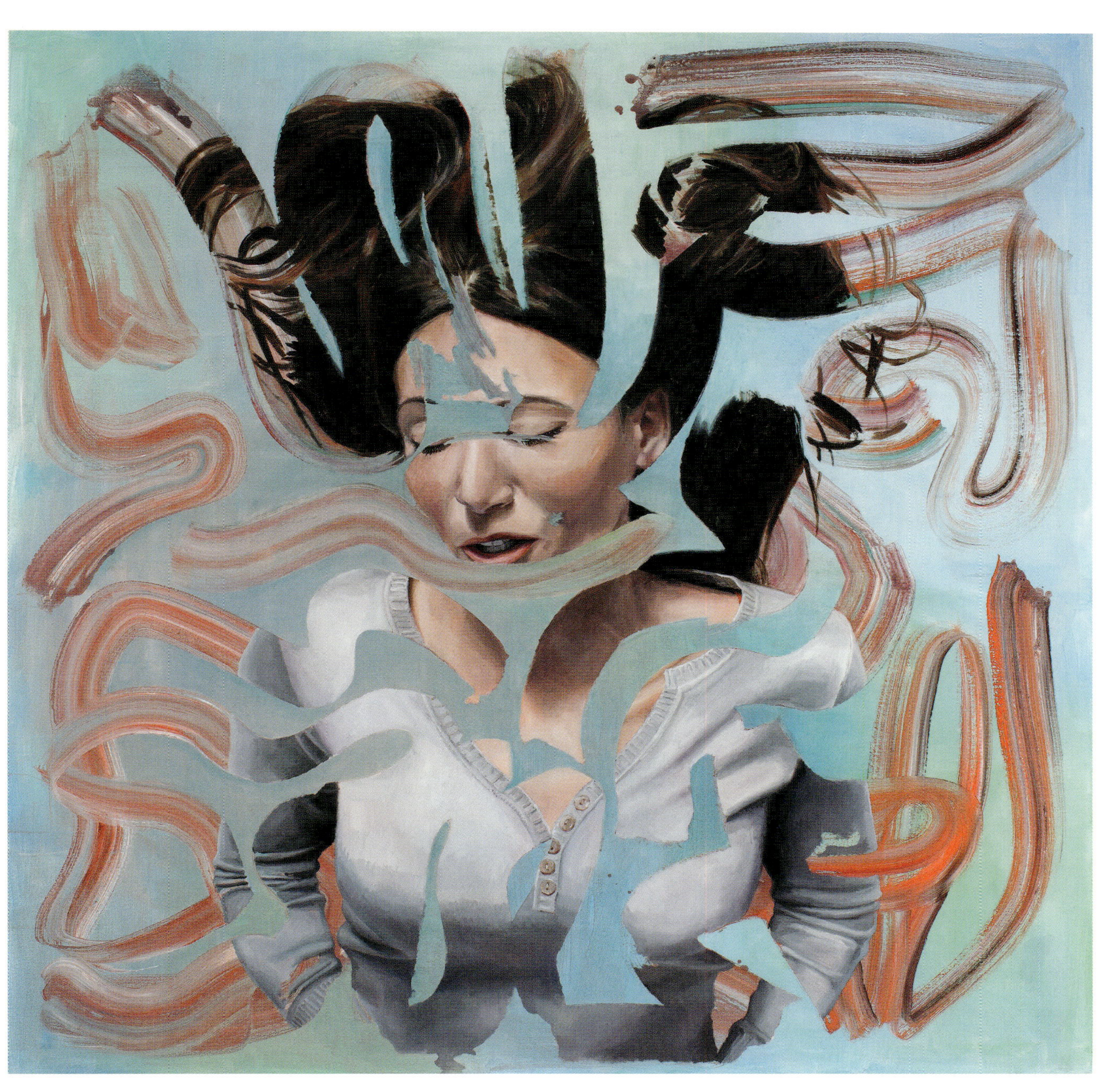

Wandering Mind 2015, 190 x 190 cm, acrylic and oil on canvas

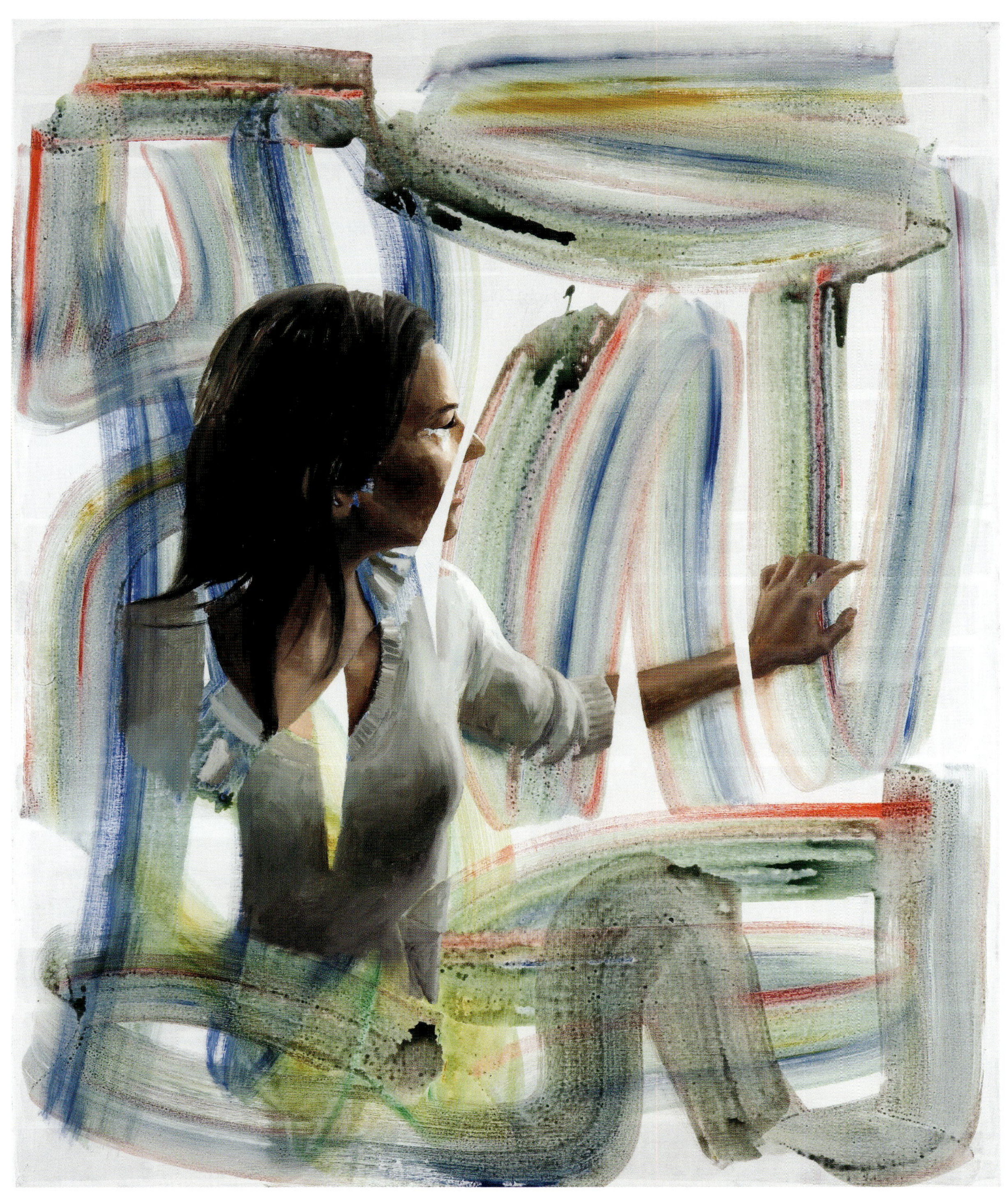

One Thought 2014, 160 x 130 cm, acrylic and oil on canvas, Daniel Sipos collection, Budapest

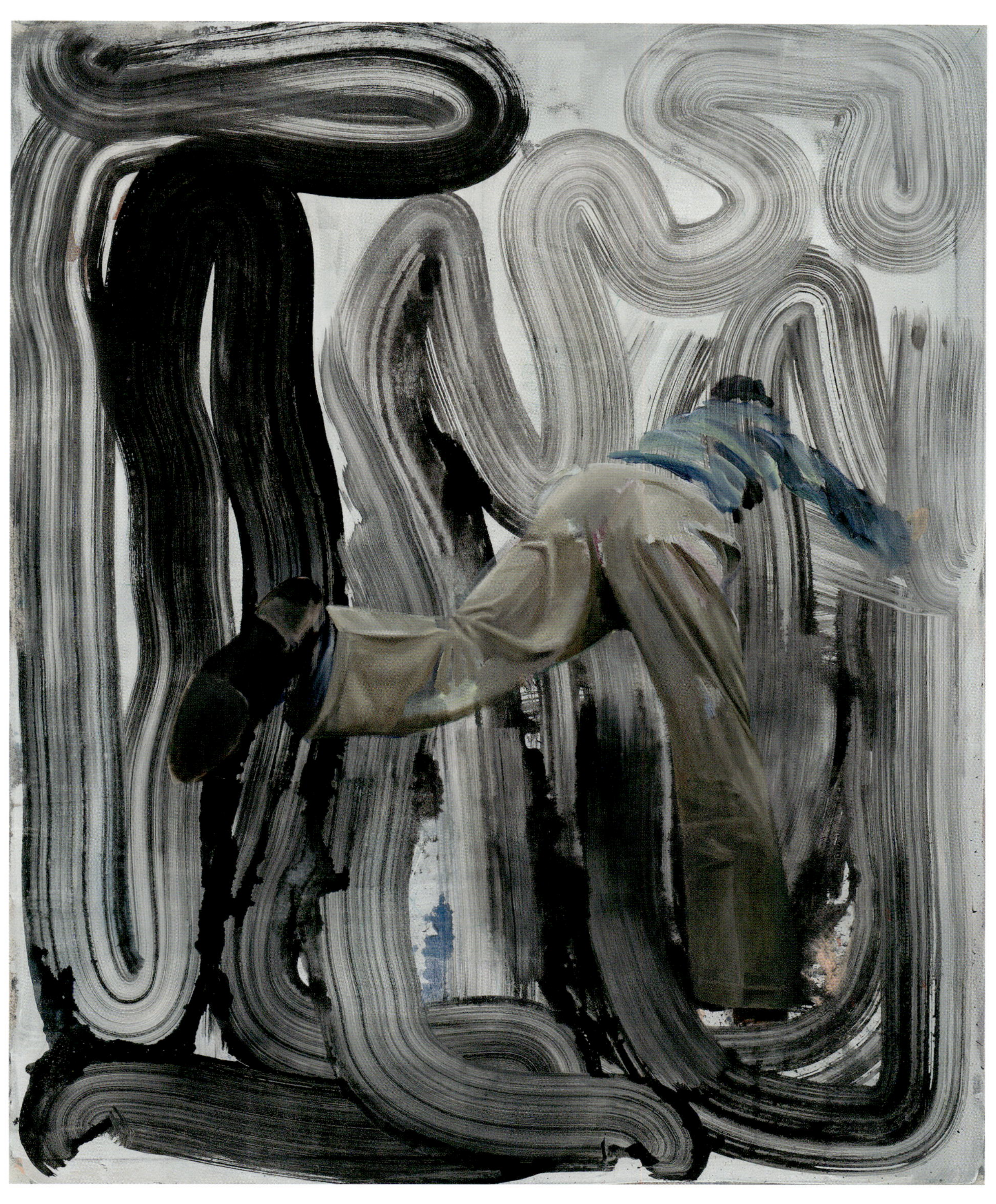

Age Dive 2016, 160 x 130 cm, acrylic and oil on canvas

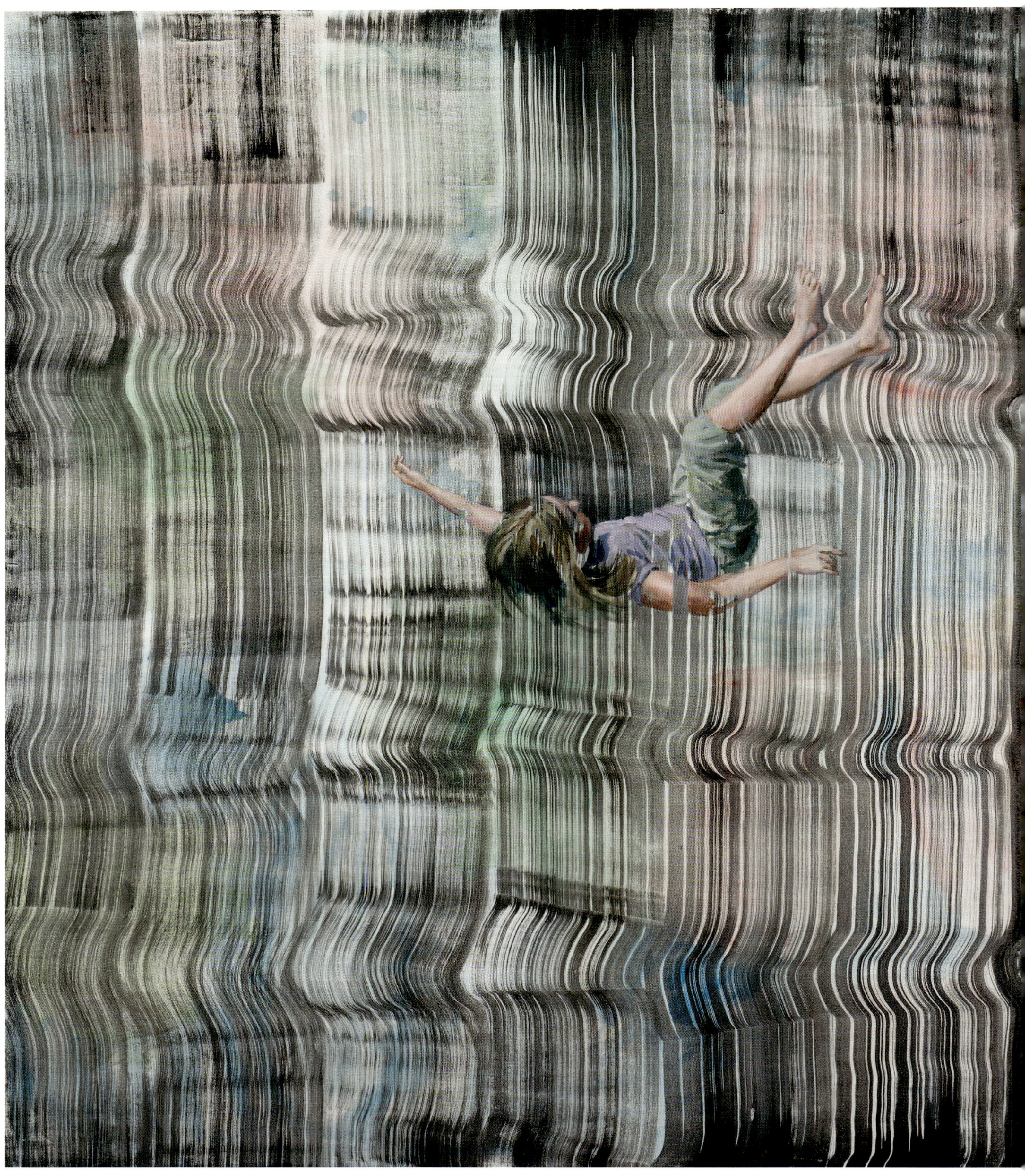

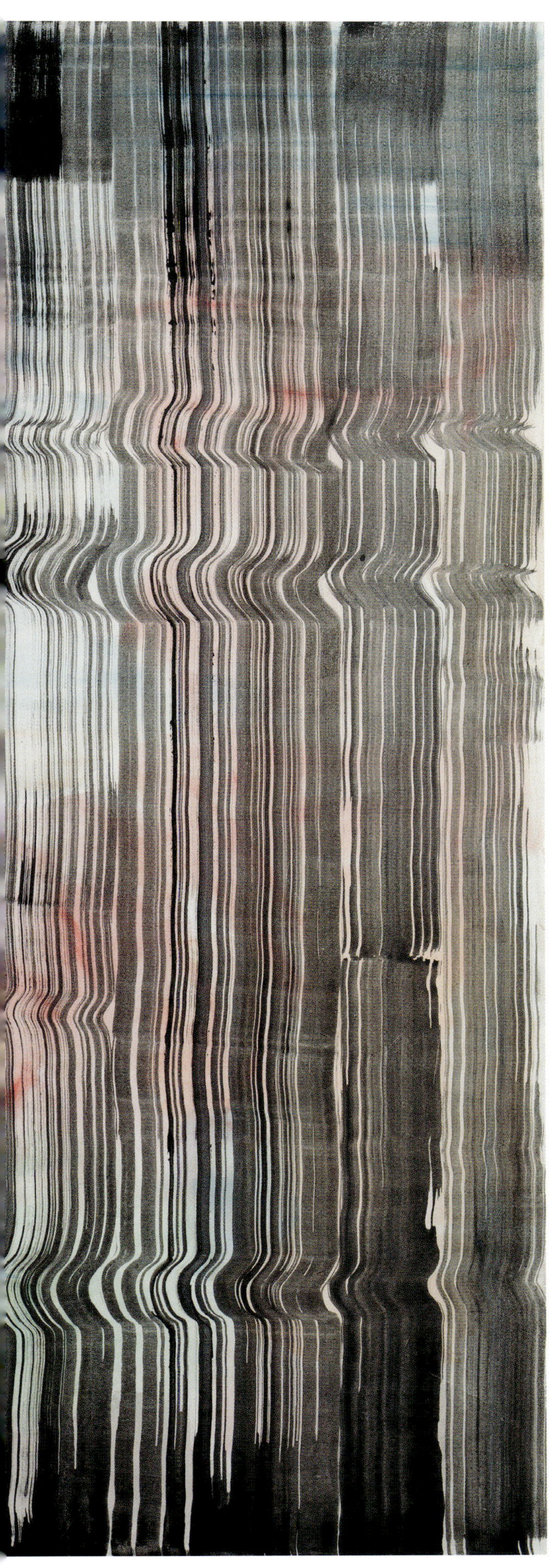

Falling Angel 2016, 160 x 200 cm, acrylic and oil on canvas

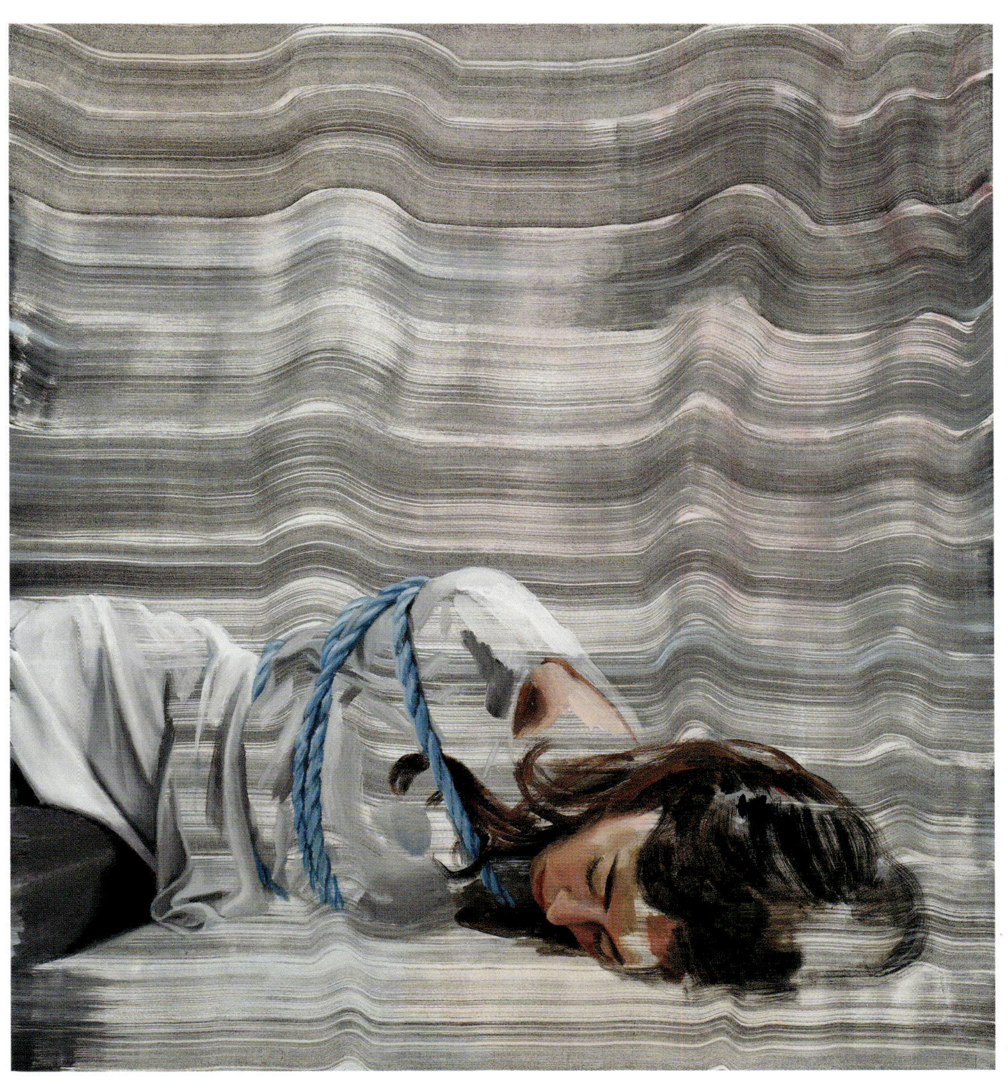

Coming Down 2016, 110 x 100 cm, acrylic and oil on canvas

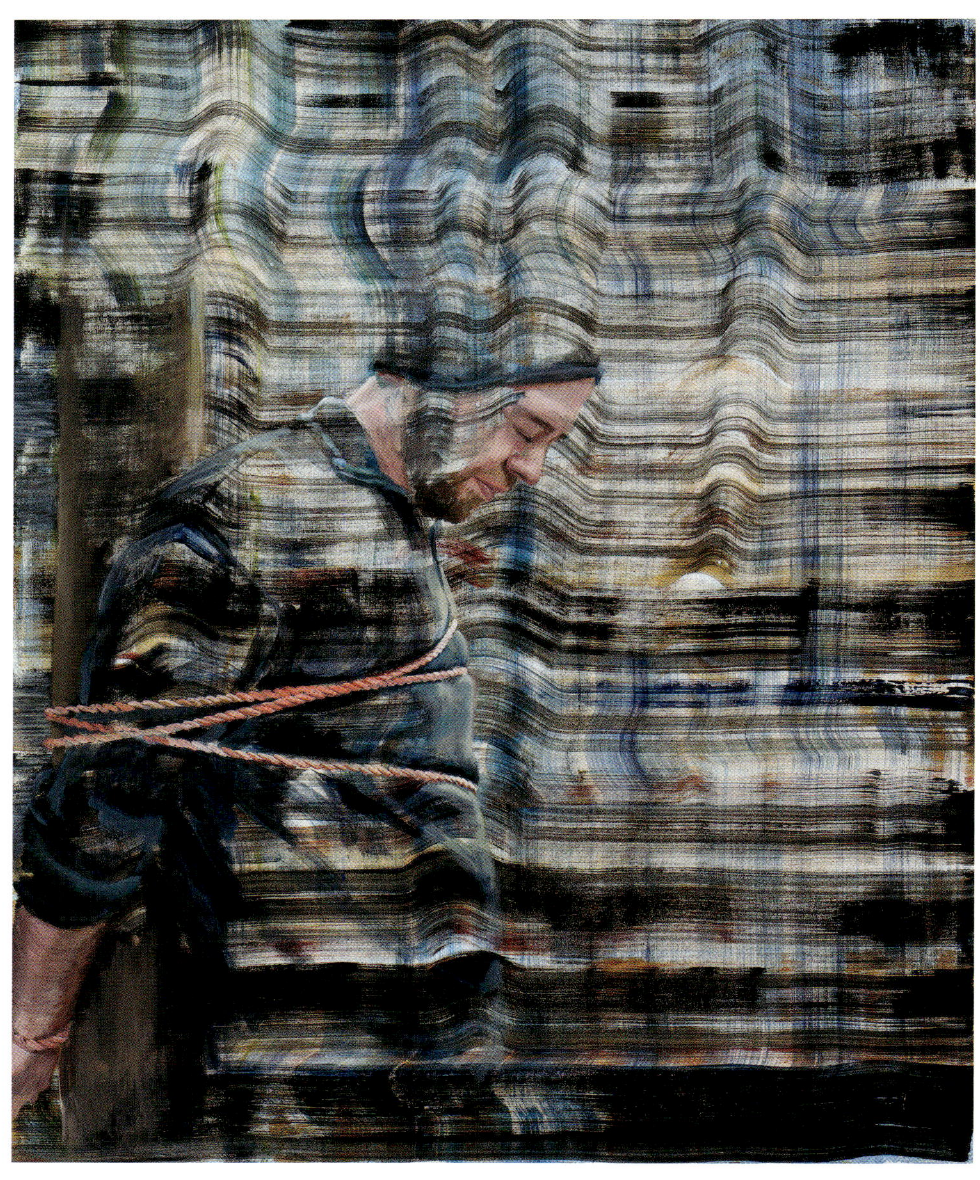

All Senses 2016, 135 x 110 cm, acrylic and oil on canvas

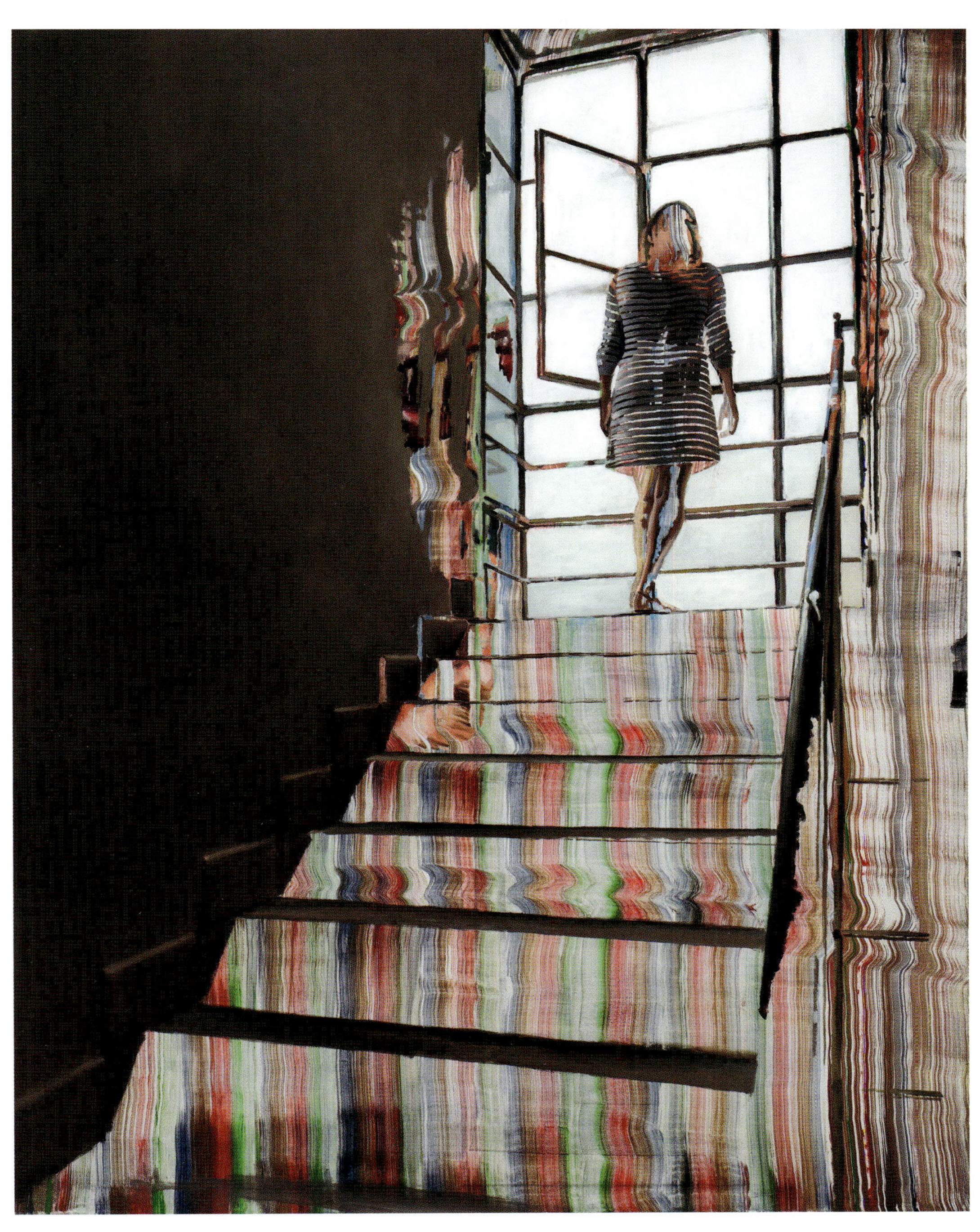

More Than Elevations 2016, 160 x 125 cm, acrylic and oil on canvas

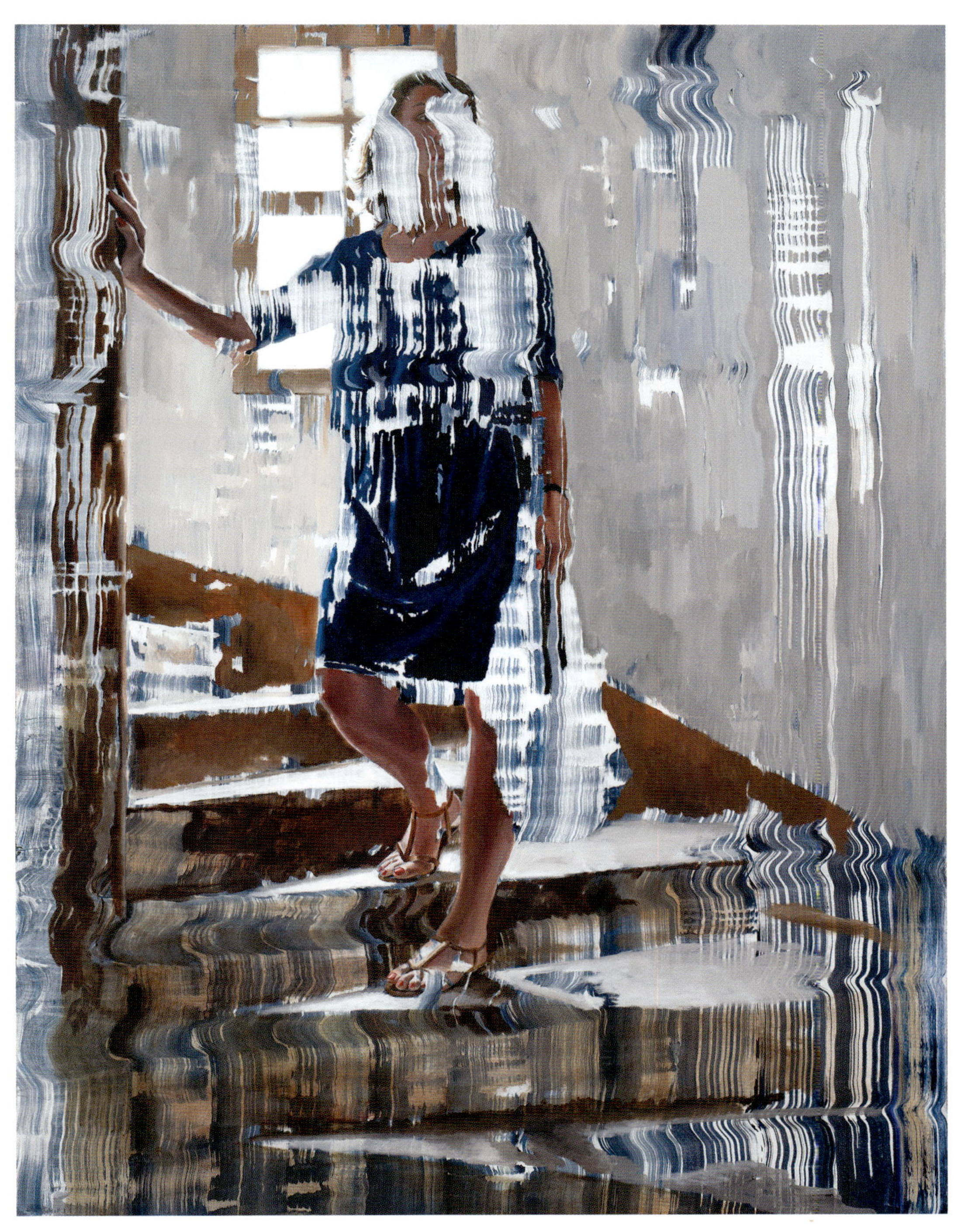

Thin Blue Pulse 2016, 165 x 125 cm, acrylic and oil on canvas

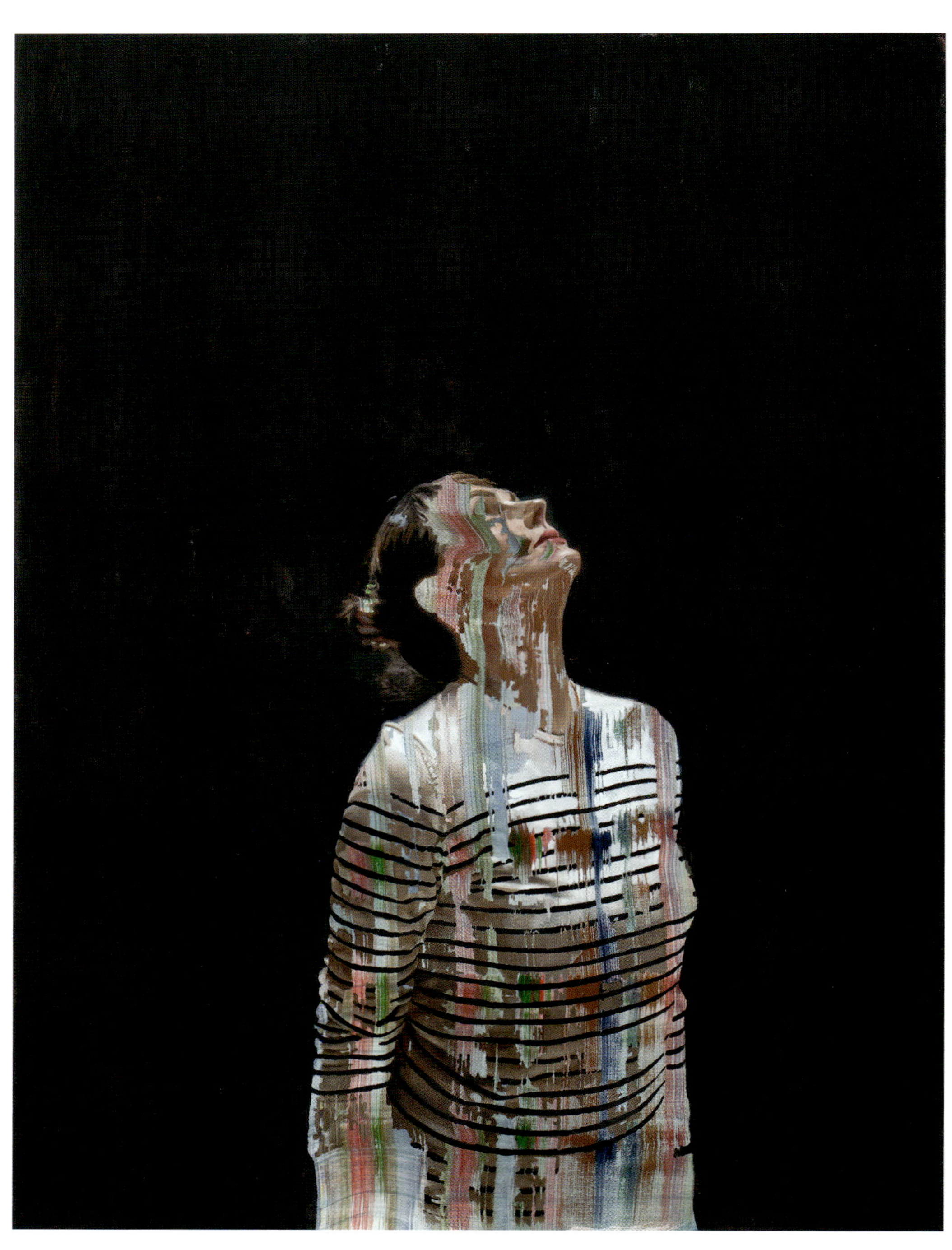

Eat My Oxygen 2016, 140 x 105 cm, acrylic and oil on canvas

1970 * Diepholz, Germany
1988-1990 studies at the Gerrit Rietveld Academy, Amsterdam
1990-1991 studies at the Art Academy, Budapest
1991-1992 studies at the St. Luc Academy, Brussels
lives and works in Berlin

Solo Exhibitions

1993 *Potatoes*, **Club of Young Artists FMK**, Budapest
New Work, **Gessmann Galerie**, Neu-Isenburg,
1994 *Ghyczy*, **Institute of Music**, Budapest
1996 *Personal Projection*, **Várfok Galéria**, Budapest
1997 *Dissolving and Congealing*, **Víziválrosi Galéria**, Budapest
Monochromes, **Várfok Galéria**, Budapest
1999 *Recent Work*, **Várfok Galéria**, Budapest
2000 *Divide*, **Illárium Galéria**, Budapest
2001 *From a Different Perspektive*, **Szinyei Szalon**, Budapest
2003 *Glass and the Maiden*, **Tragor Ignác Museum**, Vác
Vakuum – Raum, **Goethe-Institut**, Budapest
Fragile, **Erika Deák Gallery**, Budapest
Unbreakable, **Emmanuel Walderdorff Galerie**, Cologne
2004 *Between Two Worlds*, **Erika Deák Gallery**, Budapest
Reflections, **Kunstraum die Rampe**, Bielefeld
2005 *Second Layer*, **Emmanuel Walderdorff Galerie**, Cologne
2006 *Observations*, **Vizivárosi Galéria**, Budapest
(with Tibor Iski Kocsis)
2007 *Siamese Savants*, **Emmanuel Walderdorff Galerie**, Cologne
2008 *Hybriden*, **Berlin Art Scouts**, Berlin
(curated by Marc Wellmann)
Mental Collage, **Erika Deák Gallery**, Budapest
2010 *Napp und Ghyczy*, **Schreier & Von Metternich Fine Arts**, Düsseldorf (with Janetta Napp)
Mind Out Of Time, **Erika Deák Gallery**, Budapest
Tuning In, **Galerie kulturreich**, Hamburg
2012 *Soul Out*, **Art Suites Gallery**, Istanbul
Echo Vision, **Neonchocolate Gallery**, Berlin
2013 *Die Gefühlte Mitte*, **Klettgau Galerie**, Klettgau-Grießen
Chaque être *humain*, **5 Pieces Gallery**, Bern
2014 *El acto de ser*, **Alejandro Gallery**, Barcelona
Spectral, **Whiteconcepts**, Berlin (with Greg Murr)
Insight Inside, **Pantocrator Gallery**, Shanghai
Silent Mantra, **Biksady Galéria**, Budapest
Das Fremde Selbst, **Galerie Robert Eberhardt**, Berlin
2015 *Temporary Mural*, **povvera project space**, Berlin
Close Up, **Reinhardt & Partner Contemporary**, Hamburg
Fragmentiert, **Brennwald Galerie**, Kiel
2017 *Unknown Frequencies,* **Westphal Berlin**, Berlin
Between Lines, **CHB Hungarian Cultural Institute**, Berlin

Group Exhibitions

1993 *Art Jam*, **University of Economics**, Budapest
1994 *Dionysus: Art and Wine*, **Zichy Galerie**, Leiden
4 Young Hungarian Artists, **Gildewart Galerie**, Osnabrück
(with Zsófia Harmati, József A. Erdödy and Csaba Pál)
1997 *Oil on Canvas*, **Palace of Arts (Műcsarnok)**, Budapest
2000 *Art Expo-Fresh*, **Artmill**, Szentendre
Dialogue, **Palace of Arts (Műcsarnok)**, Budapest
2001 *Aritmia 9*, **Institute of Contemporary Art**, Dunaújváros
2002 *Inherited Realism*, **Municipal Gallery**, Szombathely
2003 *Portrait*, **Erika Deák Gallery**, Budapest
Cream 2003, **MEO**, Budapest
2004 *Mediafactory: Interface*, former **Zsolnay Factory**, Pécs
Technorealism?, **Institute of Contemporary Art**, Dunaújváros
2005 *Analogue*, **Szinyei Szalon**, Budapest
2006 *Figure & Space*, **Vonderbank Galerie**, Berlin
2007 *Ungarischer Sommer*, **Kunstraum B**, Kiel
Junge Kunst aus Ungarn, **die Drostei**, Pinneberg
Life Spotting, **Vonderbank Galerie**, Berlin
(with Jörg Lohse and Anne Wölk)
2008 *10 Years*, **Erika Deák Gallery**, Budapest
Fragile Welten, **Galerie im Park**, Bremen
(with Anja Fußbach, Peter Hampel and Philip von Mentzingen)
2009 *Host Culture*, **Vízivárosi Galéria,** Budapest
2010 *I'm Not There*, **CHB Hungarian Cultural Institute**, Berlin
(with Simone Haack, Alejandro Rodriguez-González, Steffi Stangl, and Attila Szücs, curated by Uwe Goldenstein)
On Paper, **Erika Deák Gallery**, Budapest
2011 *Technology Won't Save Us*, **Art Suites Gallery**, Istanbul
Young European Landscape, **CHB Hungarian Cultural Institute**, Berlin and **Galerie Wolfsen**, Aalborg, Denmark
Ungarische Gegenwartskunst aus Berlin, **Hungarian Embassy**, Berlin (with Gábor A.Nagy, Adam Bota, and Konstantin Déry)
NordArt, **Kunstwerk Carlshütte**, Büdelsdorf
2012 *I'm Sorry, I Couldn't Recognize You*, **Port-Art Gallery**, Ankara
Schatzlager, **Emmanuel Walderdorff Galerie**, Cologne
2013 *Viel Zu Viel*, **Galerie Baum Auf Dem Hügel**, Berlin
2014 *Sunland,* **ENPC Free Trade Zone**, Shanghai
Drive the Change, **100 Plus**, Zürich
(curated by Annette von Spesshardt Portatius)
Frühjahrsausstellung, **Klettgau Galerie**, Klettgau-Grießen
(with Nina Nolte and Marco Reichert)
2016 *Millerntor Gallery #6*, **Millerntor Gallery**, Hamburg
Innerscape, **Treptower**, Berlin
Widerkunst, **Holzmarkt**, Berlin
Blick zurück - nach vorn, **Westphal Berlin**, Berlin

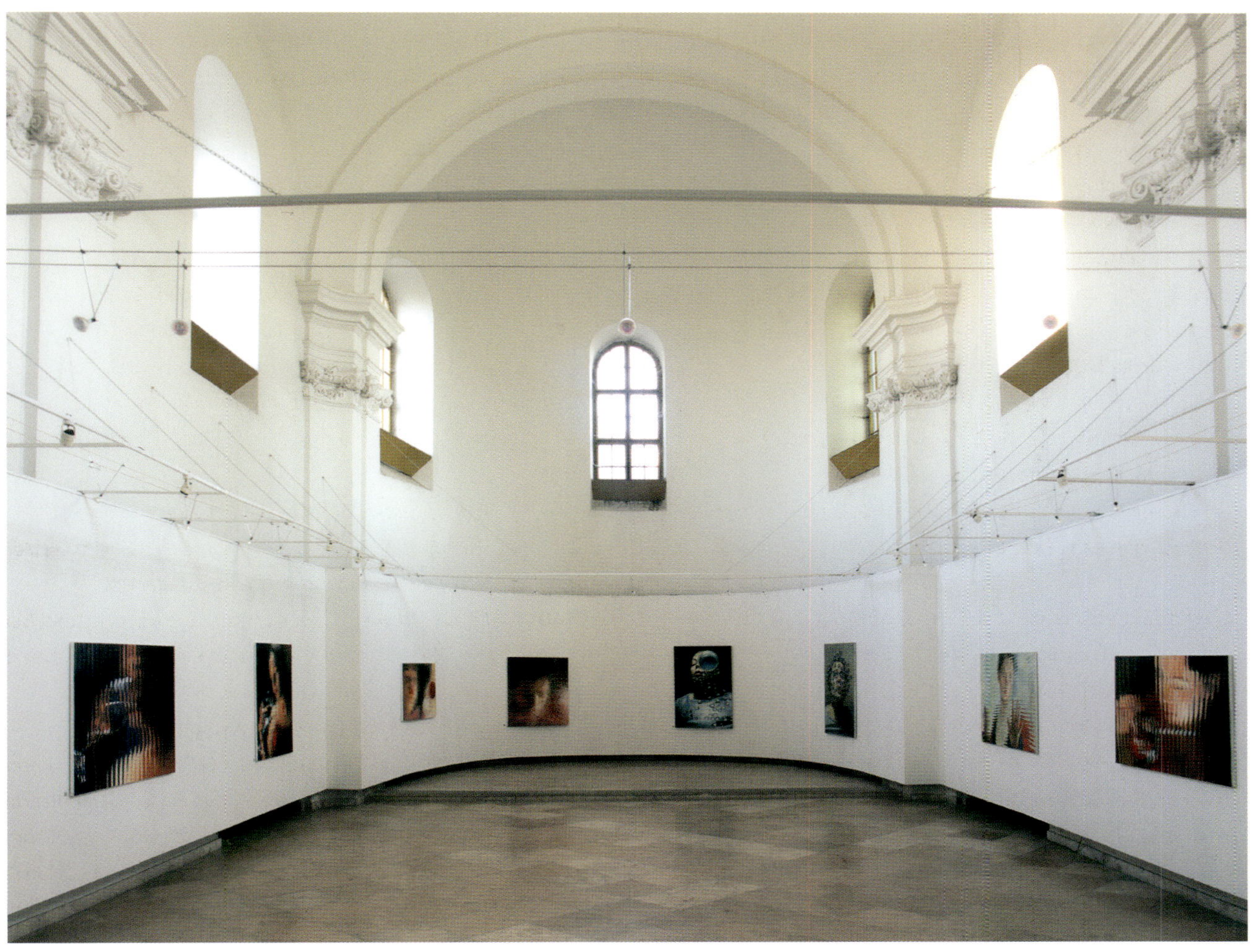

Tragor Ignác Museum, Vác 2013

Diese Publikation erscheint anlässlich der Ausstellung:
This publication was published to accompany the exhibition:

Between Lines, Collegium Hungaricum, Berlin 2017

Herausgeber / Editor:
Rabbitstreet

Endkorrektorat / Proofreading:
Ilka Backmeister-Collacott
Erik Smith

Übersetzung / Translation:
Craig Meulen

Projektmanagement / Project Management Kerber Verlag:
Kathleen Herfurth

Gestaltung / Design:
László Nádler

Besonderen Dank / Special thanks:
Jeanette Neuendorf

Für weitere Information / For more information: www.dghyczy.com

Die Deutsche Nationalbibliothek verzeichnet diese Publikation in der Deutschen Nationalbibliografie; detaillierte bibliografische Daten sind im Internet über http://dnb.dnb.de abrufbar.
The Deutsche Nationalbibliothek lists this publication in the Deutsche Nationalbibliografie; detailed bibliographic data are available on the Internet at http://dnb.dnb.de.

Gesamtherstellung und Vertrieb / *Printed and published by:*
Kerber Verlag, Bielefeld
Windelsbleicher Str. 166–170
33659 Bielefeld
Germany
Tel. +49 (0) 5 21/9 50 08-10
Fax +49 (0) 5 21/9 50 08-88
info@kerberverlag.com

Kerber, US Distribution
D.A.P., Distributed Art Publishers, Inc.
155 Sixth Avenue, 2nd Floor
New York, NY 10013
Tel. +1 (212) 627-1999
Fax +1 (212) 627-9484

Kerber-Publikationen werden weltweit in führenden Buchhandlungen und Museumsshops angeboten (Vertrieb in Europa, Asien, Nord- und Südamerika). / *Kerber publications are available in selected bookstores and museum shops worldwide (distributed in Europe, Asia, South and North America).*

ISBN 978-3-7356-0307-4
www.kerberverlag.com

Printed in Germany